Floating Home

Cyril Ionides, J. B. Atkins

B I B L I O L I F E

A FLOATING HOME

BY

CYRIL IONIDES AND J. B. ATKINS

WITH ILLUSTRATIONS BY

ARNOLD BENNETT

PHOTOGRAPHS, APPENDIX, GLOSSARY, ETC.

LONDON

CHATTO & WINDUS

1918

To
THE MATE

PREFACE

THE authors owe to their readers an explanation of the manner of their collaboration. The owner of the Thames sailing barge, of which the history as a habitation is written in this book, is Mr. Cyril Ionides. ' I ' throughout the narrative is Mr. Cyril Ionides ; the ' Mate' is Mrs. Cyril Ionides ; the children are their children. Yet the other author, Mr. J. B. Atkins, was so closely associated with the events recorded—sharing with Mr. Ionides the counsels and discussions that ended in the purchase of the barge, prosecuting in his company friendships with barge skippers, and studying with him the Essex dialect, which nowhere has more character than in the mouths of Essex seafaring men—that it was not practicable for the book to be written except in collaboration. The authors share, moreover, an intense admiration for the Thames sailing barges, to which, so far as they know, justice has never been done in writing. Mr. Atkins, however, felt that it would be unnecessary, if not impertinent, for him to assume any personal shape in the narrative when there was little enough space for the more relevant

PREFACE

and informing characters of Sam Prawle, Elijah Wadely, and their like.

The book aims at three things : (1) It tells how the problem of poverty—poverty judged by the standard of one who wished to give his sons a Public School education on an insufficient income—was solved by living afloat and avoiding the payment of rent and rates. (2) It offers a tribute of praise to the incomparable barge skippers who navigate the busiest of waterways, with the smallest crews (unless the cutter barges of Holland provide an exception) that anywhere in the world manage so great a spread of canvas. Londoners are aware that the most characteristic vessels of their river are 'picturesque.' Beyond that their knowledge or their applause does not seem to go. It is hoped that this book will tell them something new about a life at their feet, of the details of which they have too long been ignorant. (3) It is a study in dialect. It was impossible to grow in intimacy with the Essex skippers of barges without examining with careful attention the dialect that persists with a surprising flavour within a short radius of London, where one would expect everything of the sort—particularly in the *va-et-vient* of river life—to be assimilated or absorbed.

As to (1) and (3) something more may be said.

One of the authors (J. B. A.) published in the *Spectator* before the war a brief account of

PREFACE

Mr. Cyril Ionides' floating home, and was immediately beset by so many inquiries for more precise information that he perceived that a book on the subject—a practical and complete answer to the questions—was required. Neither of the authors is under any illusion as to the determination of those who have made such inquiries. Most of the inquirers no doubt are people who will not go further with the idea than to play with it. But that need not matter. The idea is a very pleasant one to play with. The few who care to proceed will find enough information in this book for their guidance. The items of expenditure, the method of transforming the barge from a dirty trading vessel into an agreeable home, a diagram of the interior arrangements, are all given. The castle in Spain has actually been built, and people are living in it.

Here is a scheme of life for which romantic is perhaps neither too strong a word nor one incapable of some freshness of meaning. The idea is available for anyone with enough resolutior Of course, not every amateur seaman would car to undertake the mastership of so large a vess as a Thames sailing barge, but that natural hesitation need be no hindrance. The owner would want no crew when safely berthed for the winter ; and in the summer a professional skipper and his mate (only two hands are required) would sail him about with at least as much satisfaction to him as is

PREFACE

obtained by the owners of large yachts carrying bloated crews.

If he is a 'bad sailor' he could get more pleasure from a barge than from an ordinary yacht of greater draught. The barge can choose her water ; she can run into the smooth places that lie between the banks of the complicated Thames estuary. She can thread the Essex and Suffolk tidal rivers ; the Crouch, the Roach, the Blackwater, the Colne, the Stour, the Orwell, the Deben, the Alde, are all open to her, and are delightfully wild and unspoiled ; she can sit upright upon a sandbank till a blow is over. Many people who could afford yachting and are drawn to it persistently think that it is not for them, because they are 'bad sailors.' If they tried barging on the most broken coast in England—say between Lowestoft and Whitstable —they would be very pleasantly undeceived, unless indeed their case is hopeless. This book, however, is not written to recruit the world of yachtsmen, but to show how a home—a floating home on the sea for winter as well as summer, not a tame house-boat—and a yacht may be combined at a saving of cost to the householder.

And by those whose heart is equal to the adventure this cure for the modern 'cost of living' will not by any means be found an uncomfortable make-shift, a disagreeable sacrifice by a conscientious father of a family. A barge is not a poky hole.

PREFACE

The barge described in this book, though one is not conscious of being cramped inside her, is only a ninety tonner. It would be easy to acquire a barge of a hundred and twenty tons, and such a vessel could still be sailed by two hands. The saloon in Mr. Ionides' barge is as large as many drawing-rooms in London flats which are rented at £150 a year. In a small London flat which was not designed for inhabitants ' cooped in a wingèd sea-girt citadel ' (though it might have been better if it had been) there is little thought of saving space. In a vessel, one of the primary objects of the designer is to save space. Sailors in their habits act on the same principle. The success that has been achieved by both archi-tects and seamen is almost incredible. No one who has lived for any length of time in a vessel has ever been able to rid himself of the grateful sense that he has more room than he could have expected, and certainly more than ever appeared from the out-side.

Nor do the points in favour of a vessel as a house end there. A ship is cool in the summer and warm in the winter. In the summer you have the sea breezes, which can be directed or diverted by awnings and windows as you like. In the winter a ship is easily warmed and there are no draughts. Although a vessel is farther removed from the world than a flat, your contact with the world is paradoxically closer. If you go downstairs from your flat you must dress

PREFACE

yourself for the street. The very man who works the lift, and mediates between you and the external world, expects it of you. But from your comfortable cabin on board ship to the deck, which gives you a platform in touch with all that is outside, there are but half a dozen steps up the companion. And yet, in touch with the world, you are still in your own territory. You have not, as a matter of habit, changed your clothes.

A sea-going vessel is a real home, a property with privileges attached, and a solution of a difficulty. We hear much praise of caravanning—a most agreeable pastime for those who prefer the rumble of wheels to the wash of the tide or the humming of wind in the rigging. But is it a solution of anything? It has not been stated that it is. Let any receiver of an exiguous salary, who trudges across London Bridge daily between his train and his office, not assume finally that a more romantic way of life than his is impossible. Let him lean for a few moments over the bridge, watch the business of the Pool, and ask himself whether he sees in one of the sailing barges his ideal home and the remedy for him of that tormenting family budget of which the balance is always just on the wrong side.

Life in a barge brings you acquainted with bargees. They are your natural neighbours. The dialect of those who belong to Essex has been reproduced in this book as faithfully as possible. If certain words

PREFACE

such as 'wonderful' (very) and 'old' occur very frequently, it is because the authors have written down yarns and phrases as they heard them, and not with an eye to introducing what might seem a more credible variety of language. It is said that dialects are everywhere yielding to a universal system of education. In the opinion of the authors the surrender is much less extensive than is supposed. Some people have no ear for dialect, and are capable of hearing it without knowing that it is being talked. The users of local phrases, for their part, are often shy, and if asked to repeat an unusual word will pretend to be strangers to it, or, more unobtrusively, substitute another word and continue apace into a region of greater safety. The authors, however, have had the good fortune to be on such terms with some men of Essex that they have been able to discuss dialect words with them without embarrassment. It is hoped that the glossary at the end of the book will be found a useful collection by those who are interested in the subject. Some of the words, which have become familiar to the authors, are not mentioned in any dialect dictionary. Although the Essex dialect has persisted, it has not persisted in an immutable form. So far as the authors may trust their ears, they are certain that the pronunciation of the word 'old' (which is used in nearly every sentence by some persons) is always either 'ould' or 'owd.' But if one looks at the well-

PREFACE

known Essex dialect poem 'John Noakes and Mary Styles : An Essex Calf's Visit to Tiptree Races,' by Charles Clark, of Great Totham Hall (1839), one sees that 'old' used to be pronounced 'oad.' In the same poem 'something' is written 'suffin',' though the authors of this book, on the strength of their experience, have felt bound to write it 'suthen.' In Essex to-day 'it' at the end of a sentence, and sometimes elsewhere, is pronounced 'ut'—in the Irish manner. Some words are pronounced in such a way as to encourage an easy verdict that the Essex accent is Cockney, but no sensitive ear could possibly confuse the sounds. In the Essex scenes in 'Great Expectations' Dickens made use of the typical Essex word 'fare,' but he did not attempt to reproduce the dialect in essential respects. Mr. W. W. Jacobs's delightful barge skippers are abstractions. They may be Essex men, but they are not recognizable as such. Enough that they amuse the bargee as much as they amuse everybody else ; one of the authors of this book speaks from experience, having 'tried' some of Mr. Jacobs's stories on an Essex barge skipper. No more about dialect must be written in the preface. Readers who are interested will find the rest of the authors' information sequestered in a glossary.

Mr. Arnold Bennett, who has settled in Essex near the coast, and is, moreover, a yachtsman, shares the enthusiasm of the authors for the peculiar

PREFACE

character of the Essex estuaries. He makes his first appearance here as an illustrator. He has given his impressions of the scenery in which the barges ply their trade, and which is the setting of the following narrative.

It remains to say that in the narrative several names of places in Essex, as well as the real name of the barge, have been changed ; and that the authors wish to thank the proprietors of the *Evening News*, who have allowed them to republish Sam Prawle's salvage yarn, which was originally printed as a detatched episode.

ILLUSTRATIONS

I. COLOUR PLATES FROM WATER-COLOUR DRAWINGS BY ARNOLD BENNETT

II. MONOCHROME PLATES FROM PHOTOGRAPHS

A FLOATING HOME

CHAPTER I

'I will go back to the great sweet mother,
Mother and lover of men, the sea.'

ONE winter I made up my mind that it was
necessary to live in some sort of vessel afloat instead
of in a house on the land. This decision was the
result, at last pressed on me by circumstances, of
vague dreams which had held my imagination for
many years.

These dreams were not, I believe, peculiar to
myself. The child, young or old, whose fancy is
captive to water, builds for castles in Spain house-
boats wherein he may spend his life floating in his
element. His fancy at some time or other has played
with the thought of possessing almost every type of
craft for his home—a three-decker with a glorious
gallery, a Thames houseboat all ready to step into,
a disused schooner, a bluff-bowed old brig. He will
moor her in some delectable water, and when his
restlessness falls upon him he will have her removed
to another place. Civilization shall never rule him.

A FLOATING HOME

As though to prove it he will live free of rates, and weigh his anchor and move on if the matter should ever happen to come under dispute. Nor will he pay rent resentfully to a grasping landlord. For a mere song he will pick up the old vessel that shall contain his happiness. Her walls will be stout enough to shelter him for a lifetime, though Lloyd's agent may have condemned her, according to the exacting tests that take count of sailors' lives, as unfit to sail the deep seas.

Certainly those who have the water-sense, yet are required by circumstances to earn their living as landsmen, have all dreamed these dreams. In many people the sight of water responds to some fundamental need of the mind. To the vision of these disciples of Thales everything that is agreeable somehow proceeds from water, and into water everything may somehow be resolved. When they are away from water they are vaguely uncomfortable, perhaps feeling that the road of freedom and escape is cut off. Inland they will walk, like Shelley, across a field to look at trickling water in a ditch, or will search out a dirty canal in the middle of an industrial town. The sea, which to some eyes seems to lead nowhere, seems to them to lead everywhere. Iceland and the Azores open their ports equally to the owner of any kind of vessel, and the wind is ready to blow him there, house and all. The water-sense is the contradiction in many people of the hill-sense. They

A FLOATING HOME

of the water-sense cannot tolerate that too large a slice of the sky, in which they love to read the weather-signs, should be eclipsed; the wonderful lighting of the mountains is less significant to them than the marshalling of vapours and tell-tale clouds upon their spacious horizon.

But this water-sense which lays a spell on you often exacts severe tolls of labour. The yachtsman who employs no paid hands, for instance, must sweat for his enjoyment; the simple acts of keeping a yacht in sea-going order, of getting the anchor and making sail, and of stowing sail and tidying up the ship when he has returned to moorings, mean exacting and continuous work. If he goes for a short sail the labour might reasonably be said to be disproportionate to the pleasure ; and if he goes for a long sail the pleasure itself may easily turn into labour before the end. These disadvantages and uncertainties the yachtsman knows, and yet they are for him no deterrent. He may spend a miserable night giddily tossed about in an open and unsafe anchorage, and call himself a fool for being there ; but the next week he will expose himself to the same discomfort. Why ? Because it is in his blood; because he has this water-sense which compels him, bullies him, and enthrals him.

The houseboats of the Thames are famous centres of a dallying summer existence in which life tunes itself to the pace of the drifting punts and

A FLOATING HOME

skiffs, and seems to be expressed by the metallic melody of a gramophone or the tinkling of a mandolin. At night there is enough shelter for paper lanterns to burn steadily ; and as the wind is tempered, so is everything else. All is arranged to add the practical touch of ease and comfort to the ideal of living roughly and simply, and the result is a mixture of paradox and paradise. One wonders what proportion of the population of the house-boats, if any, lives in the houseboats in the winter. The boats always seem to be empty then, and of course they were not designed for regular habitation. A wall or roof which, like

> ' The soul's dark cottage, battered and decayed,
> Lets in new light through chinks that time has made,'

is not a meet covering for the winter. Nor would even a thoroughly weather-proof boat be so if it have no fireplace. But thought runs on from the spectacle of the mere Thames houseboat to the further possibilities of this mode of life. Why keep to the tame scenes of the upper Thames ? Why not live on the Broads, under that clean vault of sky, scoured by the winds, among the wilder sights and sounds of nature ? Thought runs on again. Why on the Broads, after all ? They are a long way from London, and it may happen that one has to be often in London. And in the summer you might imagine that the upper Thames had been transported to Norfolk, so full are the Broads and

4

A FLOATING HOME

rivers of picnicking parties. Why, then, not live in a houseboat on sea water? Sea water is a great purifier. No fear that it will become stagnant or rank. Its transmuting process turns everything to purity. Take an odd proof. Even rubbish or paper in sea water is not an offence as it is in fresh water. Hurried along on the tide, it bears a relation to the great business of ships; but in fresh water it reminds one of disagreeable people, careless of all the amenities.

The houseboat, then, must be a ship lying with her sisters of the sea in a harbour. Attracted by the Government advertisements that appear from time to time in shipping newspapers, one thinks, perhaps, or buying an old man-of-war. But old men-of-war, though very roomy, are more expensive than you might suppose. Besides, in the conditions of sale there may be a stipulation that the buyer must break up the ship. A barque, such as is often bought by a Norwegian trader in timber, and spends her remaining days being pumped out by a windmill on deck, might serve for a houseboat. So would a steam yacht when the engines had been taken out. But then the draught of either is not light, and the occupier of a houseboat might want to lie far up a snug creek, and there even the highest spring tide would not give him the necessary depth. A sea houseboat might be built specially, but that is not the way of wisdom; the cost would be very great. The houseboat must be a

A FLOATING HOME

vessel of very easy draught, and also one that can be bought cheap and be easily adapted for the purpose.

Often had my thoughts carried me to this point by some such stages as have been described. But the floating home had remained a phantom because my desire for the sea was partly satisfied by the possession of a small yacht, the *Playmate*, of which I was the Skipper and my wife was the Mate, and in which we had spent all our holidays. Our home was a country cottage, which I had bought at Fleetwick, not far from a tidal river that strikes far into the heart of Essex. But at length circumstances, as I have said, caused the dream to become for me a very practical matter.

It happened in this way. The shadow of the change from governess to school had fallen on our two boys. We regretted it the more because there was no school within reach of home, and they were, in our opinion, too young to go to a boarding school. And so there seemed nothing to be done but to sell or let our cottage—if we could—where we had lived for nine years, and move to some place where there was a good school for the boys. Whatever place we chose had to be on or near salt water, for neither my wife nor I could seriously think of life without water and boats.

We found a satisfactory school near a tidal river in Suffolk, but we could not find a house—at least, not one we both liked and could afford. One day,

A FLOATING HOME

having returned dejectedly from a search as futile as usual, we were discussing the situation, which indeed looked hopeless, for our means were obviously unequal to what we wanted to do, when the idea of a floating home suddenly repossessed me with a fresh significance.

' Let's buy an old vessel,' I said, ' and fit her up as our house. We have often talked of doing it some day. That may have been a joke, perhaps. But why not do it *seriously—now ?*'

The Mate evaded the startling proposal for the moment.

' I wish the children wouldn't grow up,' she commented sadly.

' If we don't have the vessel,' I persisted, ' we shall fall between two stools, because with all the expenses—school, rent, and so on, which we've never had before—we shall have to give up the *Playmate.*'

' That would be worse than anything.'

The mere idea of giving up our boat was more than we could contemplate—our boat in which we two had cruised alone together, summer and winter, on the East Coast, and from whose masthead more than once we had proudly flown the Red Ensign on our return from a cruise ' foreign.'

' I would rather live in a workman's cottage and keep the boat, than live in a better house and have no boat,' said the Mate emphatically.

7

A FLOATING HOME

'Well, we've got to leave here, and it's something to have found a decent school. I suppose, if we take a house really big enough to hold us, it will cost us forty pounds to move into it.'

'*Much* more than that if you count all the new carpets, curtains, and dozens of other things we shall want.'

I thought an occasion for reiteration had arrived.

'Just think. If we had a ship, we should do away with the expense of moving for one thing, the rent for another, and the rates and taxes for another. We may be absolutely sure our expenses will increase, and our income almost certainly won't.'

The Mate was silent, so I continued : 'Suppose we are reduced to doing our washing at home. Washing hung up to dry in the garden of a villa is one thing, but slung between the masts of a ship it is another. Not many people can scrub their own doorsteps without feeling embarrassed, but one can wash down one's own decks proudly in front of the Squadron Castle.'

'There is something in that.' She was gazing out over the marshes, where the gulls and plover were circling. She sighed, and I knew she was thinking of the 'move.'

I sat beside her and looked out of the window too, and the familiar sight of a barge's topsail moving above the sea-wall caught my eye. 'That's what we should be doing,' I said, pointing to the

A BARGE AT SUNSET IN THE LOWER THAMES

A FLOATING HOME

barge—'sailing along with our children and our household gods on board instead of waiting for pantechnicons to arrive with our furniture, and spending days in misery and discomfort moving it into a house we don't like, and then paying a large rent every year for the privilege of staying in it. If we had a barge we could anchor clear of the town, and when the holidays came we could up anchor and clear off to a place more after our own hearts. Of course a barge is the very thing—the most easily handled ship for her size in the world. I see the way out quite clearly now.'

'Yes, that sounds very jolly, but there would be a lot of drawbacks too.' The Mate began to retreat towards the drawing-room.

'Oh, but you haven't heard half the advantages yet,' I called after her.

The Mate wanted time. So did I. I lit a cigarette and thought for a few minutes over our position; and the more I thought the more sure I became that a barge would solve the problem for us. And when I joined her I felt that I had a pretty strong case.

'Now listen to me,' I said. 'Not only should we save a great deal over the move, and over the rates and taxes, and have no landlord to interfere with us, but we should actually be freer than we are here. We should be sure of our sailing, which is one great advantage; and later, when the boys go to their public school, we can move wherever we like

9

and not be tied to a house for seven, fourteen, or twenty-one years. A move without a move—think of that. I am sure salt-water baths will be good for the children, and hot salt-water baths will be excellent for rheumatism—or anything of that sort. The barge will be warmer in the winter than a house, and cooler in the summer. She will be cheaper to keep up. You will save in servants and also in coals. You know you hate tramps, and hawkers, and barrel-organs. Well, you will be free from all these things. Of course, we don't have earthquakes in England, but if we did have one we shouldn't feel it. If we had a flood, it wouldn't hurt us. You remember we paid about four pounds to have our burst water-pipes mended last winter, but we shouldn't have that sort of thing in a barge. We shouldn't be swindled over a gas-meter, and servants wouldn't leave because of the stairs. It will be a delightful place for the children to bring their friends to, and no one will know whether we're eccentric millionaires or paupers only just to windward of the workhouse. We'll have the saloon panelled in oak, and white enamel under the decks, and our books and blue china all round. We'll . . .'

I had just begun to warm to my work when an expression on the Mate's face showed me that I had said enough and said it reasonably well. I had made an impression on her adventurous heart.

CHAPTER II

'Come with me from Lebanon, my spouse, with me from
    Lebanon,
Down with me from Lebanon to sail upon the sea.
The ship is wrought of ivory, the decks of gold, and thereupon
Are sailors singing bridal songs, and waiting to cast free.

'Come with me from Lebanon, my spouse, with me from
    Lebanon,
The rowers there are ready and will welcome thee with shouts.
The sails are silken sails and scarlet, cut and sewn in Babylon,
The scarlet of the painted lips of women thereabouts.'

Two or three days after the conversation related in
the last chapter the Mate and I fell into a vein of
reminiscence and reconstructed a vision we had
once shared of the ship that was some day to be
our home. It had the proper condition of a vision
that the thing longed for was unattainable; the
vessel of our dreams had always been as far down
on the horizon as the balance at the bank that
would pay for her.

She was, above all things, to be beautiful, even
for a ship, which is saying much—for who ever
saw a sailing ship otherwise? Of course, she was to
be square-rigged, for how else should we be able to

splice the mainbrace with rum and milk when the
sun crossed the yard-arm? We fancied gorgeous
pictures on her sails, so that the winds should be
lovesick with them as with the sails of Cleopatra's
barge; an ensign aft, and streaming pennants of
bright colours on her masts. Her poop, towering
above the water, fretted and carved and blazoned
with all the skill of bygone guilds, should have a
gallery aft on which the captain and his wife
would take their ease On either quarter, lit up at
sundown, there would be tall poop lanterns covered
with cunning tracery and magic, such as Merlin
might have wrought, so that on windy nights the
passing craft might see

'Far, far up above them her great poop lanterns shine,
Unvexed by wind and weather, like the candles round a Shrine.'

Guns she would have on deck, and a fighting-top
on the main, and a forecastle where the crew
should man the capstan and weigh anchor to a
chanty. Beneath her jibboom pointing heavenward
she would set a spritsail heralding her on her way.
We could see her with sails all bellied out in bold
curves before a brave wind, and hear 'the long-
drawn thunder neath her leaping figure-head.'
    Thus she would sail on her happy course, leaving
behind ' a scent of old-world roses.' She would have
to return, though, amid the smell of burnt crude
oil or coal, for of course she could never go to

A FLOATING HOME

windward. And I am afraid we were going to have electric light too. After all, we are practical people.

I remember the evening of this reminiscence very well, because I suddenly became conscious that we were talking of the vision as a thing that had been supplanted by something else. There was no doubt about it. Our remarks had implied our consent to the scuttling of that glorious galleon. We took an artistic interest in the image, but it was no longer even good make-believe.

The more I had thought over it the more the idea of the barge had taken hold of me as a feasible scheme, for I was almost sure that the sale of the cottage and the *Playmate* would realize enough to buy the barge and pay for making her habitable.

I was familiar with the dimensions of a barge, and sketched out roughly to scale various plans by which we could have five sleeping cabins, a saloon, a dining cabin, kitchen, scullery, forecastle, and steerage. This occupation became so fascinating that I could hardly tear myself away from it at nights to go to bed.

As I am inclined to be the fool who rushes in while the Mate is the angel who fears to tread, it was natural for her to maintain certain objections for some time, even though thus early I could see that she was nearly as much bitten by the thought of the barge as I was. Here is the kind of discussion that would occur:

A FLOATING HOME

Skipper : You see, we've only got to be tidy and there'll be heaps of room.

Mate : You don't understand. Men never do. There are hundreds of things one doesn't want in a yacht, even on a long cruise, which one must have in a house-boat.

Skipper : Well, there'll be our cabin and a cabin for the boys, and another for Margaret, a spare cabin, the saloon, the dining-room, the bathroom, the kitchen, the forecastle, the steerage, and lots of lockers and cupboards everywhere.

Mate : Oh, you don't understand.

Skipper : I could be bounded in a nutshell and feel myself the king of infinite space.

Mate : Hamlet won't help us !

Skipper : But look at the alternative. If we go in for a house and can't afford the rent we shall have to give up the *Playmate* and take to walks along a Marine Parade instead. Oh, Lord !

Mate : The children might fall overboard.

Skipper : We can have stanchions all round the ship and double lines.

Mate : What about slipping overboard between the ropes ?

Skipper : Well, I don't want to be laughed at, but if you really wish it we'll have wire netting as well.

Mate : What about a water-supply ? We can't get on without plenty of fresh water.

14

A FLOATING HOME

Skipper : You shall have plenty.

Mate : How ?

Skipper : In huge tanks.

Mate : What shall I do without my garden ?

Skipper : That is the worst point and the only bad point. I've got no answer except that we must give up something, and the question is whether you would rather have the garden than everything else. Oh, happy thought !—some day we will tie up alongside a little patch and cultivate it.

Mate : Are you perfectly sure we shan't have to pay rates ?

At this point the Skipper could always cite in evidence the case of the ' floating ' boathouse near by, which had been rated because it would not float. That proved to demonstration that anything capable of floating would not have been rated. Our friend Sam Prawle, an ex barge skipper, who lived in an old smack moored on the saltings, held himself an authority on rating in virtue of having taken part in this case. He had helped to build the floating boathouse, and therefore felt that his credit was involved in her ability to float.

Some years ago our saltings—the strip of marsh intersected by rills, which is covered by water only at spring tides—were not considered to have any rateable value. Later a good many yachts were laid up on them, and as the berths were paid for the saltings were rated. Then followed two or three

A FLOATING HOME

small wooden boathouses on piles, in which gear was kept, and on these a ferret-eyed busybody cast his eye. He reported them as being of rateable value. It was argued that the boats in which gear was stored, as distinguished from the yachts, might as well be rated too; but this would not hold water, for the simple reason that boats could be floated off and anchored in the river or taken away altogether, whereas the boathouses, though often surrounded by water, were buildings on the land.

To avoid paying rates, therefore, and at the same time to have a comfortable place in which to camp out and store things, the yacht-owner who employed Sam Prawle decided to build a floating boathouse. Sam and he, having fixed several casks in a frame, built a house on this platform.

Now it came to pass that the local ferret informed the overseers that this ' building on the saltings ' did not float, and was therefore rateable. From that time onwards until the matter was decided our waterside world argued about little else but whether it was a house-boathouse or a boat-househouseboat. The owner was invited to meet the overseers at the next spring tide to satisfy them on the point.

Sam worked hard all the morning of the trial, covering the casks with a thick mixture of hot pitch and tar. A small crowd gathered on the sea-wall to watch events. It was a good tide, and I, who was

present as chairman of the overseers, was glad,
because it gave the owner a fair run for his money.
My sympathy was all with him, although as an
official I had not been able to give him the benefit
of the doubt. As the tide rose near its highest point
Sam and the owner, wading up to their thighs in
sea-boots, did their utmost to lift the boathouse or
move her sideways, but without success.

At the top of the tide, both of them, red in the
face and sweating hard, managed to raise one end a
couple of inches, and called on Heaven and the
overseers to witness that the boathouse floated. As
chairman of the overseers, I took the responsibility
of saying that if they could shift her a foot sideways she should be deemed to have floated. They
went at it like men, but the tide had fallen an inch
before their first effort under these terms was ended,
and two or three minutes later Sam was heard to
say to the owner, ' That ain't a mite o' use a shovin'
naow, sir. She's soo'd a bit.'

And so the boat-houseboat turned out to be a
house-boathouse after all, and was assessed at £1 a
year. Sam used to pay the rate every half-year on
behalf of his employer, not without giving the
collector his views on the subject.

When the Mate had been convinced that we
should really escape rates the thought of giving up
her garden remained the last outwork of her very
proper defences. But this position also fell in good

17   C

time. My foot-rule, my rough scale plans and piled-up figures of cubic capacity and surficial area carried all before them. I trembled for my arithmetic once or twice, however, when I proved that we should have very nearly as much room as in the cottage.

A barge, then, it was to be. Not a superannuated, narrow, low-sided canal barge ; nor a swim-headed dumb barge or lighter, such as one can see any day of the week bumping and drifting her way up and down through London—the jellyfish of river traffic ; nor yet, above all, an upper Thames houseboat of any sort, but a real sailing Thames topsail barge which could work from port to port under her own canvas, and meet her trading sisters in the open on their business.

* * * * *

The news that we were going to live in a barge spread like wildfire, and raised a storm of protest which took all our seamanship to weather. Many a time I had to clear off the land, so to speak, against an onshore gale with my barge and family. We thought our relations were unreasonable, for all barge skippers to whom we unfolded our plan became enthusiastic and said—tactful men !—that their wives were of the same mind. I claimed their views as expert at the time, though to be sure I knew well enough that there is a law of loyalty among sailormen whenever the old question of wives sailing with their husbands is discussed.

A FLOATING HOME

Our relations, who did not know a Thames topsail barge from a Fiji dug-out, regarded our scheme alternately as a sign of lunacy and as an injury to themselves. They were bent on shaking us; third parties were suborned to try tactfully to dissuade us, leading up to the subject through rheumatic uncles on both sides of the family. The emissaries lacked versatility, for they all approached the subject by way of uric acid, and the moment we heard the word rheumatism we took the weather berth by saying in great surprise, 'You've come to talk about the barge, then?'

Having outsailed the emissaries, we were still bombarded with letters mentioning every possible objection. One said the barge would be dark, and we replied that we intended to have twenty-six windows. Another that it would be damp; against this we set our stoves. Another that it would be stuffy; and the windows were indicated once more. A fourth that it would be cold; and we brought forward the stoves again. A fifth declared that it would be draughty. To this last we intended to reply at some length that a ship with her outer and inner skin, and air-lock or space between the two, is the least draughty place possible. On second thoughts, however, we felt it would be waste of time, so, acting the part of a clearing-house, we switched the 'draughty' aunt on to the 'stuffy' uncle and left them to settle which it was to be.

19

A FLOATING HOME

Really we were too full of hope and plans to care what anyone said. Life was not long enough to get on with our work and answer objections too, so after a time we settled down in the face of the world to a policy of masterly silence.

In the meantime, as a first step, we took the measurements of a barge lying at Fleetwick Quay, so that we knew more accurately than before what room we should have, and could plan our home accordingly.

How those winter evenings flew! Armed with rulers, pencils, and drawing-boards, we sat in front of the drawing-room fire working like mad. We used reams of paper and blunted innumerable pencils making designs of the various cabins and placing the cupboards, the bunks, the bath, the kitchen range, the water-tanks, the china, the silver, the furniture, and the thousand and one things which make a house. After we had spent a week in deciding where the various pieces of furniture were to go, we discovered that they could not possibly be got in through the hatchways we had planned, and we accordingly designed a special furniture hatch. It was glorious fun, and we were always springing surprises on each other, and mislaying our pencils and snatching up the wrong one in the frenzy of a new idea. Indeed, we became so much absorbed that progress was hindered, for we could not be induced to look at each other's plans

A FLOATING HOME

until we agreed to have two truces every night for purposes of comparison.

At any moment the house might be sold, and then we should want our barge, and buying a barge is not to be done in a moment or unadvisedly. The transaction is critical. We should not be able to go back upon it. Yacht copers, we knew, were as bad as horse copers, but both apparently were new-born babes compared with barge copers, if our information were correct.

CHAPTER III

' Dulcedo loci nos attinet.'

THE primitive explorers who came up the Thames in their rough craft examined the site of what was afterwards to be London, and saw that it was good. London is where it is because of the river. It is strange that Londoners should know so little, below bridges, of the river that made them. The reason, of course, is that the means of seeing it are very poor. How many Londoners could say how to come upon even a peep of the lower river within a distance of five miles of London Bridge ? The common impression is that the river is impenetrably walled up by warehouses, wharfs, docks, and other forbidden ground. A simple way is to go by steamer when steamers are plying, but the best way is to be taken on board a sailing barge.

Taine said that the only proper approach to London was by the Thames, as in no other way could a stranger conceive the meaning of London. And from the water only is it possible to see properly one of the most beautiful architectural visions in the world—the magnificent front of

A FLOATING HOME

Greenwich Hospital, rising out of the water, as noble a palace as ever Venice imagined.

If this is the most splendid spectacle of the lower Thames, the most characteristic sight is that of the sailing barges, of which you may pass hundreds between London Bridge and the Nore. These are vessels of which Londoners ought to be very proud indeed; they ought to boast of them, and take foreigners to see them. But, alas! the very word 'barge' is a symbol of ungainliness and sordidness. What beauty of line these barges really have, from the head of the towering topsail to the tiny mizzen that lightens the work of steering! There is no detail that is weak or mean; a barge thriddling (as they say in Essex) among the shipping of the winding river in a stiff breeze is boldness perfectly embodied in a human design. The Thames sailing barges are one of the best schools of seamanship that remain to a world conquered by steam.

The Thames barge is worthy to be studied for three reasons: her history, her beauty, and her handiness. She is the largest sailing craft in the world handled by two men—often by a man and his wife, or a boy—and that in the busiest water in the world.

One hundred to one hundred and twenty tons is the size of an average barge nowadays. Seventy-five to eighty feet long by eighteen feet beam are her measurements. With leeboards up she draws about three feet when light and six when loaded; when she is loaded, with her leeboards down, she draws fourteen feet.

For going through the bridges in London or at Rochester, or when navigating very narrow creeks, she will pick up a third hand known as a ' huffler ' (which is no doubt the same word as ' hoveller ')* to lend a hand.

Some explanation must be given of how it is possible for two men to handle such a craft. In the first place, the largest sail of all, the mainsail, is set on a sprit, and is never hoisted or lowered, but remains permanently up. When the barge is not under way this sail is brailed or gathered up to the mast by ropes, much as the double curtain at a theatre is drawn and bunched up to each side. The topsail also remains aloft, and is attached to the topmast by masthoops, and has an inhaul and a downhaul, as well as sheet and halyard. Thus it can be controlled from the deck without becoming unmanageable in heavy weather. It is an especially large sail, and so far from being the mere auxiliary which a topsail is in yachts, it is one of the most important parts of the sail plan, and is the best-drawing sail in the vessel. It requires none of the coaxing and trimming which the yachtsman prac-

---

* A hoveller is an unlicensed pilot or boatman, particularly on the Kentish coast. The word is said to be derived from the shelters or hovels in which the men lived, but such an easy derivation is to be mistrusted.

THE SWALE RIVER

A FLOATING HOME

tises before he is satisfied with the set of the little sail which stands in so different a proportion and relation to his other sails. Often in a strong wind you may see a barge scudding under topsail and headsails only. The truth is that when a barge cannot carry her topsail it is not possible to handle her properly. The foresail, like the mainsail, works on a horse. These and several other things too technical to be mentioned here enable the barge to be worked short-handed.

From Land's End to Ymuiden the Thames barge strays, but her home is from the Foreland to Orfordness. Between these points, up every tidal creek of the Medway, Thames, Roach, Crouch, Blackwater, Colne, Hamford Water, Stour, Orwell, Deben, and Alde, wherever ' there is water enough to wet your boots,' as the barge skipper puts it, one will find a barge.

She is the genius of that maze of sands and mud-banks and curious tides which is the Thames Estuary. Among the shoals, swatchways, and channels, she can get about her business as no other craft can. The sandbanks, the dread of other vessels, have no terror for her ; rather, she turns them to her use. In heavy weather, when loaded deep, she finds good shelter behind them ; when light, she anchors on their backs for safety, and there, when the tide has left her, she sits as upright as a church. Then, too, she is consummate in cheating the tides and making short cuts, or ' a short spit of it,' as bargees say. In this the sands help her, for the tide is far slacker over the banks than in the fairway, where her deep-draught sisters remain. While these are waiting for water she scoots along out of the tide and makes a good passage in a shoal sea.

What do all the barges carry? What do they not carry? were easier to answer. They generally start life—a life of at least fifty years if faithfully built and kept up—with freights of cement and grain, and such cargoes as would be spoilt in a leaky vessel. From grain and cement they descend by stages, carrying every conceivable cargo, until they reach the ultimate indignity of being entrusted only with what is not seriously damaged by bilge water.

Barges even carry big unwieldy engineering gear, and when the hatches are not large enough, the long pieces, such as fifty-foot turnable girders, are placed on deck. The sluices and lock-gates for the great Nile dam at Assuan were sent gradually by barge from Ipswich to London for transhipment.

Hay and straw—for carrying which more barges are used than for any other cargo except cement—must be mentioned separately. After the holds are full the trusses of hay or straw are piled up on deck to a height of twelve to fifteen feet. At a distance the vessel looks like a haystack adrift on the sea. The deck cargo, secured by special gear, often weighs as much as forty tons, and stretches

A FLOATING HOME

almost from one end of the ship to the other. There is no way from bow to stern except over the stack by ladders; the mainsail and foresail have to be reefed up, and a jib is set on a bowsprit; and the mate at the wheel, unable to see ahead, has to steer from the orders of the skipper, who 'courses' the vessel from the top of the stack. To see a 'stackie' blindly but accurately turning up a crowded reach of London River makes one respect the race of bargees for ever. How a 'stackie' works to windward as she does, with the enormous windage presented by the stack, and with only the reduced canvas above it, is a mystery, and is admitted to be a mystery by the bargemen them-selves. One of them, when asked for an explanation, made the mystery more profound by these ingenuous words : ' Well, sir, I reckon the eddy draught off the mainsail gits under the lee of the stack and shoves she up to wind'ard.'

The Thames barge is a direct descendant of the flat-bottomed Dutch craft, and her prototype is seen in the pictures of the Dutch marine school of the seventeenth century. Both her sprit and her lee-boards are Dutch; the vangs controlling the sprit are the vangs of the sixteenth-century Dutch ships; and until 1830 she had still the Dutch overhanging bow, as may be seen in the drawings of E. W. Cooke. The development of her—the practical nautical knowledge applied to her rigging and gear

A FLOATING HOME

—is British, like the invincible nautical aplomb of her crew.

Those who have watched the annual race of the Thames barges in a strong breeze have seen the perfection of motion and colour in the smaller vessels of commerce. The writer, when first he saw this race and beheld a brand-new barge heeling over in a wind which was as much as she could stand, glistening blackly from stem to stern except where the line of vivid green ran round her bulwark (a touch of genius, that green), with her red-brown sails as smooth and taut as a new dog-skin glove, and her crew in red woollen caps in honour of the occasion, exclaimed that this was not a barge, but a yacht.

A barge never is, or could be, anything but graceful. The sheer of her hull, her spars and rigging, the many shades of red in her great tanned sails, the splendid curves of them when, full of wind, they belly out as she bowls along, entrance the eye. Whatever changes come, we shall have a record of the Thames barge of to-day in the accurate pictures of Mr. W. L. Wyllie. He has caught her drifting in a calm, the reflection of her ruddy sails rippling from her; snugged down to a gale, her sails taut and full, and wet and shining with spray; running before the wind; thrashing to windward with topsail rucked to meet a squall; at anchor; berthed. Loaded deep or sailing light; with tower-

A FLOATING HOME

ing stacks of hay; creeping up a gut; sailing on blue seas beneath blue skies; or shaving the countless craft as she tacks through the haze and smoke of a London reach, she is always beautiful.

Of course the bargees pay their toll of lives like other sailors. They are not always in the quiet waters of liquid reflections that seem ·to make their vessels meet subjects for a Vandevelde picture. Many stories of wreck, suffering, and endurance might be told, but one will suffice—a true narrative of events. The barge *The Sisters*, laden with barley. screenings, left Felixstowe dock for the Medway one Friday morning. She called at Burnham-on-Crouch, and on the following Friday afternoon was between the Maplin Sands and the Mouse Lightship, when a south-west gale arose with extraordinary suddenness. Before sail could be shortened the topsail and jib were blown away. The foresail sheet broke, and the sail slatted itself into several pieces before a remnant could be secured. Under the mainsail and the remaining portion of the foresail the skipper and his mate steered for Whitstable. Then the steering-chain broke, and nothing could be done but let go the anchor. They were then in the four-fathom channel, about three-quarters of a mile inside the West Oaze Buoy.

The seas swept the barge from end to end. Darkness fell, and for an hour the skipper burnt flares, while his mate stood by the boat ready to cast it off from the cleat in an emergency. The emergency came before there was a sign of approaching rescue. The barge suddenly plunged head first and disappeared. The mate, with the instinct of experience, cast off the painter of the boat as the deck went down beneath his feet. Both men went under water, but the boat was jerked forwards from her position astern as the painter released itself, and the men came up to find the dinghy between them. It was a miracle, but so it happened. They grabbed hold of her before she could be swept away, climbed in, and began to bail out the water. With one oar over the leeside and the other in the sculling-hole they made for the Mouse Lightship. 'If we miss that,' said the skipper, 'God knows where we shall go!' For four hours they struggled towards the Mouse light, although they could not always see it, and eventually came within hailing distance. They shouted again and again, but the crew of the lightship, though they heard them, could not at first see them. At last the boat came near enough for a line to be thrown across it. The boat was hauled alongside and the men were drawn up into safety, 'eaten up with cramp,' as the skipper said, and numb with exhaustion and exposure. At the same moment the boat, which was half-full of water, broke away and disappeared.

Perhaps the best time to see a barge is while,

A FLOATING HOME

deep laden, she beats to windward up Sea Reach,
on a day when large clouds career across the sky,
sweeping the water with shadows, as the squalls
boom down the reach, and the wind, fighting the
tide, kicks up a fierce short sea. Then, as the fishermen say, the tideway is ' all of a paffle.' As the barge
comes towards you, heeling slightly (for barges
never heel far), you can see her bluff bows crashing through the seas and flinging the spray far
up the streaming foresail. It bursts with the rattle of
shot on the canvas. You can see the anchor on the
dripping bows dip and appear as sea after sea thuds
over it, and the lee rigging dragging through the
smother of foam that races along the decks and
cascades off aft to join the frothy tumult astern.
You can see the weather rigging as taut as fiddle-
strings against the sky. Now she is coming about!
The wheel spins round as the skipper puts the helm
down, and the vessel shoots into the wind. She
straightens up as a sprinter relaxes after an effort.
The sails slat furiously ; the air is filled with a
sound as of the cracking of great whips ; the sprit,
swayed by the flacking sails, swings giddily from
side to side ; the mainsheet blocks rage on the horse.
Then the foresail fills, the head of the barge pays
off, and as the mate lets go the bowline the stay-
sail slams to leeward with the report of a gun. The
mainsail and topsail give a last shake, then fill with
wind and fall asleep as the vessel steadies on her

course and points for the Kentish shore. As she heels to port she lifts her gleaming side and trails her free leeboard as a bird might stretch a tired wing. She means to fetch the Chapman light next tack.

A fleet of barges shaking out their sails at the turn of the tide and moving off in unison like a flock of sea-birds is a picture that never leaves the mind. And darkness does not stop the bargeman even in the most crowded reaches so long as the tide serves. Every yachtsman accustomed to sail in the mouth of the Thames has in memory the spectral passing of a barge at night. She grows gradually out of the blackness. There is the gleam of her side light, the trickling sound of the wave under her forefoot, the towering mass of sombre canvas against the sky, the faint gleam of the binnacle lamp on the dark figure by the wheel, the little mizzen sail right aft blotting out for a moment the lights on the far shore, and the splash-splash of the dinghy towing astern. There she goes, and if the fair wind holds she will be in London by daybreak.

CHAPTER IV

'And sometimes I think a soul was gi'ed them with the blows.

WHEN the barge *Osprey* berthed at Fleetwick Quay to unload stones for our roads we went on board, and took our old friend Elijah Wadely, the skipper, into our confidence.

' Ef yaou're a goin' to buy a little ould barge, sir,' said Elijah, ' what yaou wants to know is 'er constitootion. My meanin' is, ef yaou knaow who built she, yaou'll know ef she was well built; and ef yaou knaow what trade she's bin' in you can learn from that. Naow ef she's a carryin' wheat, or any o' them grains, what must be kept dry, yaou'll knaow she can't be makin' any water, or *do*, she 'ouldn't be a carryin' 'em. Then agin, water don't improve cement, and that's a cargo what's wonnerful heavy on a barge is cement, and ef bags is spoilt that's a loss to the skipper, that is. So you can take it that barges what carry same as grain and oilcake and cement and bricks and such-like is mostly good too.

' And when yaou knaows what she's bin a carryin' yaou wants to know where she's bin a carryin' it to; for some berths is good and some is

A FLOATING HOME

wonnerful bad, specially draw-docks,* and what sort of condition she's in is all accordin' to where she's bin a settin' abaout. I've knaowed many a barge strain herself settin' in a bad berth, whereas a barge of good constitootion settin' in the same berth will maybe wring a bit and make water for a trip or two, but she'll take up agin. Yes, sir, ef yaou're a goin' to buy a little ould barge—and there ain't a craft afloat as 'ud make a better 'ome, as my missis 'as said scores o' times—yaou must study 'er constitootion.'

'How's trade, Lijah ?'

'Well, sir, I've bin bargin' forty years, and I don't fare to remember when times was so bad in bargin' afore.'

'What do you think we could get a decent 120-ton barge for, Lijah, supposing we wanted a big one ?'

'I doubt yaou 'ont get 'un under five or six hundred paounds. Yaou see, sir, what bit o' trade there is them bigger barges same as 120 tons and up'ards gits, for they on'y carries two 'ands same as we, what can on'y carry 95 ton, though by rights they ought to carry a third 'and.'

'Do you think we could get a sound 90 tonner for two hundred pounds, because that's the size we've practically decided on ?'

* Berths on the river bed, where carts come alongside at low water to unload the barges.

A FLOATING HOME

'1 don't want to think nawthen about that, I *knaow* yaou can. Why, on'y last week the *Ada* was sould for one 'undred and sixty pound, as good a little ould thing as any man ever wanted under 'im. But yaou wants to be wonnerful careful-like in buyin' a barge. Yaou know that, sir, as well as I do, and my meanin' is there's barges and barges. As I was a tellin' yer, yaou wants to know her constitootion first, and then yaou wants to knaow her character. Yaou don't want to take up with a craft what yaou can't press a bit, or what'll bury 'er jowl or keep all on a gnawin' to wind'ard or 'ont lay at anchor easy or is unlucky in gettin' run into.'

'Why, you're not superstitious, are you, Lijah?'

'No, no, sir. I'm on'y tellin' yer there's barges and barges. Look at this little ould *Osprey*, sir. Yaou can see she's got a new bowsprit. Well an' that's the third time she's bin in trouble since yaou've knaowed she, ain't it? We'd just come off the loadin' pier at Southend to make room for another barge, and we layed on that ould moorin' under the pier right agin the foot of the beach ready for the mornin's high water. Well, she took the graound all right, for she d'ent on'y float there about faour hours out of the twelve, and I went belaow to turn in for a bit. She 'adn't barely flet when I felt her snub, and there was a barge atop 'o she and aour bowsprit gone. I knaow wessels has laid on that

ould moorin' for the last twenty year, and never
ain't heard tell of one bein' in trouble afore.

'Soon as we'd got t'other barge clear, I went up
and tould the guvnor. "Lijah," 'e says, " ef I was to
put that little ould *Osprey* in my back-yard she'd
get run into." Yes, that's the truth, that is ; you can't
leave that ould barge anywhere, no matter where
that is, but the ould thing'll have suthen atop o' she.
And what's more, the guvnor's lost every case he's
took up on 'er so far, though he was allus in the
right.

'Naow the *Alma*, what my wife's cousin Bill
Stebbins is skipper of, is all the other way raound.
That ould thing's bin run into twice since Bill's had
'er, once on her transom and once on her port side
just abaft the leeboards, and there warn't no law
case nor nawthen, but each time the party what
done it agreed on a sum and paid it, and the ould
thing made money over it for 'er guvnor.

'I once see'd the *Alma* do a thing what I
wouldn't 'ave believed not if forty thaousand people
told me. She was a layin' in Limehouse reach,
stackloaded and risin' to abaout twenty fathom o'
chain. There was a strong wind daown, and she was
a sheered in towards the shore. Bill's mate was
a goin' ashore for beer, and I 'eard Bill tellin' 'im to
'urry up. I knaowed why he tould the mate to be
quick, because that blessed ould ebb was running
wonnerful 'ard, and sometimes that'll frickle abaout

A FLOATING HOME

and make a barge take a sheer aout, and p'raps break her chain, which barges do sometimes in the London River. Well, suddenly I seed that little ould *Alma* sheer right off into the river and snub up with a master great jerk what pulled her ould head raound agin. Then I see'd 'er with her chain up and daown a drivin' straight for the laower pier, where I reckoned she'd be stove in or suthen, and there was Bill alone on board as 'elpless as a new-born babe, as the sayin' is, for a' course 'e couldn't lay aout no kedge nor nawthen by 'isself.

' Well, as true as I'm a settin' 'ere that lucky ould thing come a drivin' athwart till she fetches into the eddy tide below the upper pier, and then she goes away to wind'ard, although there was a strong wind daown, mind yer, till she fetches up alongside another barge, the *Mabel*, what was a layin' there, and all Bill 'ad to do was to pass the *Alma*'s stay fall raound the *Mabel*'s baow cleat and back agin. Yes, sir, that was the head masterpiece that ever I did see.'

A few days afterwards we happened to see the *Norah Emily* down in the mouth of our river. This was the barge commanded by Bill Stebbins, the former skipper of the *Alma*. We took a rather mischievous pleasure in going on board to find out whether Bill Stebbins would confirm all Elijah had told us. We fancied that Elijah would have spoken more circumspectly about the unfailing luck of the

37

A FLOATING HOME

Alma, if he had guessed that Bill was likely to come round our way. But our doubts soon became remorse. Elijah was vindicated.

'Yes, yes,' said Bill, 'that ould *Alma* was the luckiest ould basket ever built; that d'ent matter where yaou left she, she d'ent never git into trouble. There was faour on us once't a layin' in the middle crick below the Haven, the *Lucy*, the *Susan*, the *Fanny*, and my little ould *Alma*. We had to wait our turn at the quay for loadin' straw, so the mate and me went off home for a day or two. Well, that come on to blaow suthen hard, that did, and all they there barges was in some kind of trouble, but the *Alma* she just stayed where she were and d'ent come to no manner o' harm.

'Then agin, same as in the London docks, yaou ast any barge skipper yaou like haow long a barge can lay there without a lighter or a tug or suthen wantin' she to shift. None the more for that, I've bin there plenties o' times with that little ould *Alma*, and she warn't niver in no one's way. I remember off Pickford's wharf, Charing Cross, we 'ad to shift to make room for another barge. I 'ad to goo off to fix up another freight, but reckoned to be back by six o'clock, so I tould the mate to git a hand to help shift she and make fast in case I warn't back tide-time. Well, arter I got my freight I meets one or two friends, and what with one thing and another, I den't git back till eleven o'clock o' night.

38

A FLOATING HOME

I couldn't find that mate, or, *do*, I'd a given he suthen, for there was that blessed ould thing made fast with a doddy bit o' line no bigger'n yaour finger, whereas by rights she ought to have had three or faour of aour biggest ropes to hold she from slippin' daown the wind. Anyway, there she lay end on just right for slippin' off, and niver even offered to move. As yaou knaow, sir, scores and scores o' barges 'av bruk the biggest rope they carry that way and gone slidin' daown the wind. The *Mary Jane* did, just above Bricklesey* on the way to Toozy,† and buried her ould jowl that deep in the mud on t'other side of the gut that I was skeered she wasn't goin' to fleet.

'But there y'are, that *Mary Jane* 'ouldn't never set anywhere where any other barge would ; and ef her rope was strong enough she'd have tore the main cross chock or anything else aout o' she. That's the masterousest thing, that is, but I s'pose that's all accordin' to the way her bottom is. But that ould *Alma*—well, I've heard plenties o' times afore I took she what a lucky bit o' wood she were. Look at here, sir. We was up Oil Mill Crick by Thames Haven there and the wind straight in, and us had a bit o' bad luck comin' aout, for us stuck on that slopin' shelf o' mud right agin the salts there. I felt wonnerful anxious, for there warn't three foot to spare, and ef she'd a slipped off she'd a bruk

* Brightlingsea.   † St. Osyth.

'erself to pieces. I don't reckon any other barge 'ud have hild on there, but that ould *Alma* did. She just set up there same as a cat might on a table.

' In Shelly Bay, too, just above the Chapman Light, she done a thing what no other barge 'ould have done. Us couldn't let goo our anchor where us wanted to, as there was another barge, the *Louisa*, agin the quay. I had to goo off to see the guvnor, so I ast the skipper o' the *Louisa* to give my mate a hand when the *Louisa* come off, for a course the *Alma* hadn't got near enough chain aout. Well, that bein' a calm then my mate tould the skipper o' the *Louisa* not to trouble, as he warn't goin' to shift till the mornin'. That bein' a calm then warn't to say that 'ud be a calm in the mornin'; and it warn't, for that come on to blaow a strorng hard wind straight on shore.

'That ould thing begun to drag her anchor, but as soon as ever her ould starn tailed on to that beach her anchor hild, and she lay head on to the sea as comfortable as yaou could want to be. There ain't a mite o' doubt but what ninety-nine barges out 'er a hundred 'ud have paid off one way or t'other, and come ashore broadside on and done some damage, for there's a nasty swell comes in there.'

*　　　*　　　*　　　*　　　*

Barges came and went in our river. We inspected some at the quay, and sailed down in the *Playmate*

BARGES AT AN ESSEX MILL

A FLOATING HOME

to talk to the skippers of others. We soon learned enough about barges to fill a book. We heard how the day the *Invicta* was launched she ran into another vessel and her skipper's hand was badly cut; how his wife tried (in the Essex phrase) to 'stench' the bleeding; how the skipper swore that the ship would be unlucky, as blood had fallen on her on the day she was launched; and how the wife herself died on board on the third trip. We heard of good barges and bad, of lucky barges and unlucky; of barges that would always foul their anchors, and others that never did; of barges that would carry away spars or lose men overboard, or break away from their berths, and of others that were as gentle as doves.

It seemed that barges are much like human beings; when young, they can stand strains and do heavy work which they have to give up when middle-aged. If they have a weakness of constitution it reveals itself when they are young; but having passed the critical age, they settle down to a long useful life, and it is not uncommon for them to be still at work after fifty or sixty years. But the most important result of our researches was the universal opinion that a sound 90 tonner was to be got at our price.

At least, that was the most important fact from my point of view; but I ought in truthfulness to say that while I had been making notes likely to

help me to buy a good barge with a sound constitution, the Mate had looked upon our accumulated
information from a different angle, and had been
giving her attention to barges' characters.

I might have foreseen this, for she always looked
on the *Playmate* as a living thing. She has the
feeling of the bargemen, who say of an old vessel,
'Is she still alive ?' I was not prepared, however,
for her to tell me that, however sound a barge
might be, I was not to buy her unless her character
was good. I argued in vain.

' Do you think I would be left with the children
on board a barge like the *Osprey*, always being run
into ? Or like the *Mildred*, always dragging her
anchor ? Or the *Charlotte*, who has thrown two
men overboard ? Not I !'

I pointed out that she had so successfully acquired
the spirit of barging that she was evidently made
for the life. The suggestion was received with
favour. We were indeed now so deep in the business
that we were beyond recall. Nothing remained
but to choose our particular 90 tonner with a good
character.

CHAPTER V

'Ships are but boards, sailors but men ; there be land-rats and water-rats, land-thieves and water-thieves.'

THE next thing that happened was that we received an offer of £375 for our cottage. After an attempt to 'raise the buyer one'—an attempt that would have been more persistent had our desire to become barge-owners been less ardent—we accepted the offer. We ought to have got more, but as the barge market was flat we salved our consciences on the principle that what you lose on the swings you gain on the roundabouts.

We entered the barge market as buyers. It is impossible to 'recapture the first fine careless rapture' of those days. In every 90-ton barge we looked on we saw the possible outer walls of our future home. The arrival of the post had a new significance, for we had made known far and wide the fact that we were serious buyers. We turned over our letters on the breakfast-table every morning like merchants who should say, 'What news from the Rialto ?'

43

A FLOATING HOME

The first barges we heard of were, according to the advertisement, the ' three sound and well-found sailing barges, the *Susan*, the *Ethel*, and the *Providence*, of 44 tons net register.' Each of these was about 90 tons gross register, and at that moment of optimism the chances seemed at least three to one that one of them would suit us.

Let it be said here that the net registered tonnage of barges is a conventional symbol. Whether a barge carries 100 or 120 tons, the net tonnage is always 44 and so many hundredths—often over ninety hundredths. If by any miscalculation in building she works out at 45 tons or more, a sail-locker or some other locker is enlarged to reduce her tonnage, for vessels of 45 tons net register and upwards have to pay port dues in London.

It is, of course, the ambition of every owner, whether of a 5-ton yacht or the *Leviathan*, to get his net registered tonnage as low as possible, so as to minimize his port and light dues. One well-known yachtsman who was having his yacht registered kindly assisted the surveyor by holding one end of the measuring tape. In dark corners the yachtsman could hold the tape as he pleased, but in more open places the surveyor's eye was upon him. The result was curious; the yacht turned out to have more beam right aft than amidships. 'She's a varra funny shaped boat,' said the surveyor doubtfully. Luckily his dinner was waiting for him, and

44

he did not care to remeasure a yacht about the precise tonnage of which no one would ever trouble himself.

We hurried off to consult Elijah Wadely about the *Susan*, the *Ethel*, and the *Providence*.

'Not a one o' they 'on't suit yaou, sir,' said Lijah. 'That little ould *Susan* was most tore out years ago—donkeys years ago. And that ould *Ethel* —well, she's only got one fault.'

'What's that?'

'She were built too soon,' chuckled Lijah. 'And that ould *Providence* is abaout the slowest bit o' wood ever put on the water. No, no, sir; none o' they 'on't do.'

We were disappointed, of course, but not long afterwards we heard of another barge laid up near a neighbouring town, and went to see her. She had been tarred recently and looked fairly well, but we did not trust the owner. Not long before he had tried to sell us an old punt (also freshly done up) for twenty-five shillings—a punt which we discovered had been given to him for a pint of beer. We looked over the barge accompanied by the owner, who rather elaborately pointed out defects, which he knew, and we knew, were unimportant, in a breezy and open manner, as one trying to impress us with his candour.

When the Mate was out of hearing he used endearing and obscene language about the barge, as one who should say, ' Now you know the worst of her and of me.' However, the memory of the punt, and what Falstaff describes in Prince Hal's eyes as ' a certain hang-dog look,' convinced us that the barge would never stand a survey, and we learned afterwards that she was as rotten as a pear below the water-line.

We had hardly returned from this inspection when we heard of three more barges to be sold. They were engaged in carrying cement to London and bringing back anything they could get, and at that moment were lying off Southwark.

We went at once to London. The next day we visited the *Elizabeth*, one of the barges, and were invited into the cabin by the skipper and his wife—not any of our Essex folk, worse luck. I began to make use of some of the knowledge I had acquired. In this I was checked by the lady of the barge, who said, ' It seems to me, mister, yer wants to know something, and if yer wants us to speak yer ought to pay yer footing.'

I sent for a bottle of gin, already painfully recognizing that looking at barges in our country was one thing, and in London another. The skipper and his wife appeared to be thirsty souls, for soundings in the bottle fell rapidly. We discussed the weather and things generally while I took stock of these people, who were to me a new and disagreeable type. I wondered whether they would be more likely

A FLOATING HOME

to speak the truth before they finished the gin—which they seemed likely to do—or afterwards. Meanwhile I looked round me.

The *Elizabeth* had a small cabin and no ventilation worth mentioning, and as the atmosphere grew thicker, in self-defence I lit my pipe. Then I tried again.

'Well, yer see, mister, it's this 'ere way. You wants to buy the barge, and if I says she's all right you buys 'er, and I lose my job; and if I says she ain't all right I gits into trouble with my guvnor.'

'Quite so,' I said, 'but the survey will show whether she is sound or not, and I want to save the expense of having a survey at all if she isn't sound. If I do have her surveyed and she is sound your owner will sell her anyhow. So you may just as well tell me.'

'D'yer mind saying all that over again?' remarked the skipper.

I did so, and the pair helped themselves to gin once more. 'What I says is this,' said the lady, 'this is very fine gin and a very fine barge.'

'Yus, the gin's all right, and so's the barge,' said the skipper, adopting the brilliant formula. 'I can't say fairer'n that, can I?'

The situation was becoming hopeless and my anger was rising, so I said curtly, dropping diplomacy, 'What I want to know is, does she leak, is she sound, what has she been carrying, where has she been trading to?'

A FLOATING HOME

'Can't say, mister. This's our first trip in 'er,' said the skipper.

'Fine gin and fine barge,' repeated the woman. We fled.

The second barge we visited was a good-looking craft, built for some special work, but she lacked the depth in her hold which we required for our furniture.

The third barge, the *Will Arding*, lay off deep-loaded in the fairway waiting for the tide to berth. The skipper was not on board, but a longshoreman in search of a drink gave me a list of public-houses where he might be found.

At the first three public-houses knots of grimy mariners had either just seen George or were expecting him every minute, and if I would wait one of them would find him. At the fourth public-house the same offer was made, and in despair I accepted it.

It required more moral courage than I possessed to wait with thirsty sailors, their mugs ostentatiously empty, without ordering drinks all round; yet, as I expected, the huntsman returned in a few minutes puffing and blowing—which physical distress was instantaneously cured by sixpence—to say that George was nowhere to be found.

With a gambler's throw, I tried one public-house not on my list, and George was not there; but as

A FLOATING HOME

usual there were those who knew where to find him if the gentleman would wait.

I never met George, and, judging by his friends, I did not want to; though, to be just, he might have been blamelessly at home all this time with his family. And there, as a matter of fact, he very likely was, for I learned later, what everyone else knew and I might have suspected, that he had been paid off, as this was the *Will Arding's* last trip before being sold.

We wandered back to the waterside and stood gazing at the slimy foreshore, the barges and lighters driving up on the muddy tide, the tugs fussing up and down, their bow-waves making the only specks of white in the gloomy scene, the bleak sooty warehouses, and the wharfs with their cranes like long black arms waving against the sky. We were declining rapidly into depression, when I saw emerging from the shadow of the bridge a stackie in charge of a tug.

How clean and dainty she looked, like a fresh country maid marketing in a slum ! Her fragrant stack of hay brought to us a whiff of the country whence she had come, and a vision of great stretches of marshland dotted with cattle, and hayricks sheltered behind sea-walls waiting for red-sailed barges to take them away.

The tug slackened speed ; the stack-barge was being dropped. She seemed familiar, and as she came nearer I saw her name, the *Annie*. Joe Applegate, the skipper, a trusted friend of ours, was at the wheel. How pleased I was now that I had spent those fruitless half-hours looking for George !

'Ain't that a fair masterpiece a seein' yaou here, sir !' shouted Joe in good Essex that raised our spirits like a bar of cheerful music. ' And haow's them little ould booeys ?'

He had come with 70 tons of hay for the London County Council horses. We were doubly glad to look on his honest face when he came on shore and told us that he knew the *Will Arding* well and had traded to this wharf for years.

' Yes, yes, sir; knaowed her these twenty years. She belongs to a friend of my guvnor's, and were built by 'is father at Sittingbourne, and 'as allus been well kep' up by 'is son. She'd be gettin' on for forty, I reckon, and a course she ain't same as a new barge, but she'll last your lifetime if you're on'y goin' to live in she and goo a pugglin' abaout on her same as summer-time and that. She'll 'ave a cargo of cement aboard naow—90 to 95 tons she mostly carry, and I ain't never heard of 'er spoiling a bag yet. She's got a good constitution, she 'as, but none the more for that yaou can watch she unloaded to-morrer if yaou've a mind to, and ef she suits yaour purpose ave 'er surveyed arterwards.'

The Mate asked about her character.

' She ain't never bin in trouble but once, that I

HAULING A BARGE TO HER BERTH

A FLOATING HOME

knaows on, and then she were run into by a ketch and got three timbers bruk on 'er port bow. No, no, sir ; there ain't nawthen agin that little ould thing.'

We seemed to be on the right tack at last. Having learned what more we could, we prepared to come to grips with the owner.

CHAPTER VI

'Sail on ! nor fear to breast the sea,
    Our hearts, our hopes, are all with thee !'

THE owner of the *Will Arding*, whom we met the
next day, was a kindly simple man who told us all
we needed to know about the vessel. We had prepared ourselves to cope with a coper of the worst
kind; but we were soon disarmed, and that not to
our detriment. He told us that the barge had just
finished her contract, and as, in his opinion, the days
of small barges were over, except in good times, he
was going to sell her, as she was barely paying her
way. He showed us the record of her trips, the
cargoes she had carried, the places she had traded
to, and the repairs done to her from time to time.

He was so agreeable that the Mate hesitated to
ask about her character, but her sense of duty pre-
vailed. One collision, in which she was not to blame,
and two fingers off the hand of one of her mates,
appeared to be the only blots on an otherwise stain-
less career. Joe Applegate had already told us of the
collision, though not of the fingers, and I hoped that
the Mate would be satisfied. And she was, when

A FLOATING HOME

she had learned that the fingers had been lost in the least ominous manner in which fingers conceivably could be lost.

Two days later we received a message that the *Will Arding* had unloaded, and was lying at Greenwich ready for us to examine her.

A more gloomy February day for our visit could hardly have been ; the wind was light and easterly, and a cold drizzle fell through the fog. The damp, however, did not touch our spirits. Even our bodies were warmed by excitement. The owner met us in his yard, and we tried to assume an indifference which probably did not deceive him.

The tide had ebbed some way, leaving the gravelly foreshore covered with black slime, and there, half afloat, half resting on the ground, and gently rocking to the wash of a passing tug, lay the *Will Arding*, with a slight cant outwards. Her annual overhaul was due in a month, the owner told us, thus explaining the condition of her paint and tar. She had been sailed to Greenwich by odd hands who had not even troubled to wash her down. Certainly she was looking her worst, but the eye of faith already saw the splendours of her resurrection.

As we went on board, the owner told us he had given instructions for one of the plugs to be lifted and water let in. The water was mixed with creosote to sweeten the bilge. It was as well that he told us this, for what we saw when we descended into the

53

hold might have daunted Cæsar. Some of the hatches were left on, and under these we took cover from the rain in the long dirty hold. She was still rocking slightly, and on the lee side black bilge water was slopping disconsolately backwards and forwards across the floor. A strong smell of creosote and smells of cement and other cargoes scarcely to be determined competed for recognition in our nostrils. The *Will Arding* seemed to have come down in the world; and this was the fact, for lately she had been sailed by men who can always be hired in the open market, but who do not look after their barges as the better class of skippers do. The best skippers had all taken up with the more modern class of large barges. The barges we had known in the country had always been scrupulously clean and tidy below. It was perhaps fortunate that our experience in the gin-drinker's cabin had revealed to us another world, and thus in some sense deadened the shock of what we saw now.

We passed to the cabin aft, and one glance told us that the grimy mariners of the public-houses had truly been the friends of the late skipper George. To say that the cabin was dirty and stuffy is to say nothing. Even the paint was greasy, and a stale smell, indescribable but unforgettable, hung in the air. George and his mate had left their bedding, presumably as not worth taking away. No doubt they were right.

A FLOATING HOME

Some old clothes, a half-empty tin of condensed milk, stale mustard in an egg-cup, some kind of grease in a frying-pan, two mugs with the dregs of beer in them, lay about ; and on the floor there were broken boots and old socks.

Returning to the hold, we took all the measurements necessary for our present purpose. We found that though the *Will Arding* had not as much headroom under her decks as we should have liked, she had enough for our piano, which was the tallest piece of furniture we intended to have on board. Moreover, we knew that barges of that size seldom have more headroom.

Still undepressed, if sobered by the prospect of the work to be done before we could possibly live on board, we went on shore to discuss the price with the owner. It was a most unpolemical discussion, and ended in my undertaking to buy the *Will Arding* for £140 subject to the surveyor's report. We agreed upon a surveyor, and the owner gave orders for the vessel to be put on the blocks at the next tide.

From this time forward the owner was unreservedly our friend, and we dreaded lest our prize should be snatched from us at the last moment by the untoward judgment of the surveyor. The owner fortified our courage by assuring us he had done all the annual overhauls and repairs for many years, and therefore it was hardly possible that the survey

would reveal anything that could not easily be put
right. Whatever the surveyor suggested he would
do, whether we bought the barge or not.

We could only await the surveyor's report as
patiently as might be, and having bade the owner
good-bye, we took one more look at the *Will Arding*
with I hardly know what thoughts in our minds.
She had canted over still further, and looked more
dingy than ever in the growing dusk as she sat in a
foreground of slime. Behind her on the wonderful
old river, now hurrying its fastest seawards in muddy
eddies, two of her sisters, their sails just drawing,
glided noiselessly past and were received into the
enveloping gloom, where the drizzle shut in the
horizon and sky and water met indistinguishably.

Then we returned to London.

* * * * *

At last—as it seemed, though it was only three
days later—the surveyor's report arrived. All was
well with the *Will Arding*, and she was, in the surveyor's private opinion, worth all the money we
were giving for her. The only defects worth speaking of were a sprung topmast and three damaged
ribs forward, but these had been strengthened by
' floating' ribs alongside.

We hurried to Greenwich and paid a deposit on
the price.

This time the *Will Arding* was on the blocks,
and a gang of men had burned off the old tar and

A FLOATING HOME

were busy tarring and blackleading her hull; her gear had been lowered, and our friend the owner was having a new topmast fitted to make all good. He had also turned his men on to replace a length of damaged rail. That was not the only thing which he did for us outside our agreement. Soon, indeed, he became almost as much interested in our scheme as we were ourselves, and we consulted him at almost every turn.

While the repairs were going on we completed the purchase; and we were profoundly conscious of the importance of the formalities which constituted us the recognized owners of 'sixty-four sixty-fourths' of the sailing barge *Will Arding*, with a registered number of our own.

Well, we were shipowners at any rate, and possessed the outer walls of our new home. And now the Mate and I found ourselves faced with a thousand unforeseen difficulties and problems, which crowded on us so thick that we scarcely knew where to begin to tackle them. This state of affairs compelled the drafting of rules of procedure, the chairman (myself) refusing motions on any point not mentioned in the agenda. Members of the Committee (the Mate) were allowed to make notes during the authorized debates on subjects to be referred to in the time set apart for general discussion. In this way our sanity was saved.

The first and most important thing was to disinfect the ship. And here the luck was with us, for next door to the yard where the *Will Arding* lay were some gas-works, the manager of which was a friend of the *Will Arding's* late owner. Our requirements were disclosed to the manager, who not only told us what disinfectant to use, but most kindly offered to have it mixed in the right proportions in one of his boilers at a nominal cost. From the boiler it could be discharged direct under pressure into the *Will Arding*. After consultation we decided to have holes drilled through the lining of the hold at regular intervals. When this had been done the *Will Arding* was berthed as near as possible to the boiler.

Eighty gallons of neat disinfectant were mixed with 800 gallons of boiling water, a hose was laid on board, and the fluid was squirted into each of the holes. By the time the last gallon was on board the disinfectant was just above the floor, but the bubbles of foam reached to the decks. This process caused intense curiosity in the yard, and there were many croakers who told us that we should never get her sweet.

The barge returned to the yard, where the various repairs went on for several days. In the meantime, being in the best market of the world, we bought the timber, panelling, bath, kitchen range, a hundredweight of nails, paint, varnish, hot-water apparatus, and the hundred and one other things we required to turn the barge into a tenantable

A FLOATING HOME

house. Now we enjoyed the advantage of all our work in the winter, for we had drawn up precise lists of the things to be bought.

We look back on those purchases with delight. It gives one a sense of real contact with the business of life to ask for the price of something f.o.b. London, on board one's own ship, and to order the goods to be sent to such and such a wharf to the sailing barge *Will Arding*. The summit of dignity was reached when I was able to tell a dealer, who was late in delivering his goods, that my ship with her general cargo on board was waiting to sail, and that if his goods were not on board that afternoon they would have to be sent by rail at his expense.

At last the repairs were finished, the general cargo was complete, and the hatches were on. As nothing would induce me to sleep in the cabin until it had been wholly cleaned, I decided not to sail the *Will Arding* to the Essex coast myself, but to have her delivered at the shipwright's at Bridgend —a place a few miles below Fleetwick on our river.

We saw the *Will Arding* get under way. She had improved vastly in appearance. The tide was on the turn, and the wind westerly ; great clouds sailed across the sky. It was a brave wind with a touch of spring in it, and it made the *Will Arding's* topsail slat furiously as the mate hoisted it to the music of the patent blocks. The brails were let go, the mainsail was sheeted home ; both men went forward, and

A FLOATING HOME

then the clank, clank, clank of the windlass fell on our ears with the sound we knew so well both by day and night. The chain was soon 'up and down,' and the foresail was hoisted and made fast to the rigging with a bowline. The *Will Arding* sheered slowly towards us with her sails full until the anchor checked her. Then swinging slowly round she came head to wind, her mainsail and foresail flapping loudly, and the mainsheet blocks crashing backwards and forwards on the main horse. When the foresail was aback the anchor was quickly broken out, and the barge filled on the other tack and gathered way.

We watched her standing over towards the opposite shore, until the mate got the anchor catted. Then bearing away with her great sprit right off and a white wave under her fore-foot, our home fled down the river.

BRADWELL CREEK

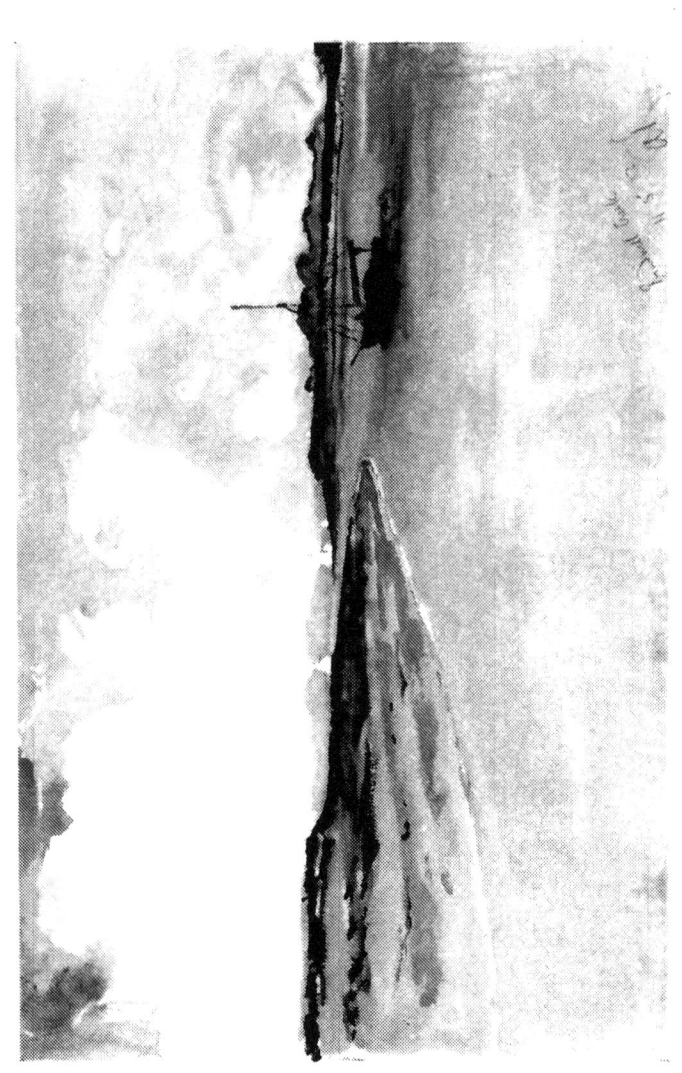

CHAPTER VII

Chantyman. Leave her, Johnny, and we'll work no more.
Chorus. Leave her, Johnny, leave her !
Chantyman. Of pump or drown we've had full store.
Chorus. It's time for us to leave her.

THE wind hung mostly west and south, and was southerly enough at the end to make the *Will Arding's* passage a fast one, and bring her early on the tide to Bridgend. There by noon next day we were looking seaward with our glasses. Shortly after that time two specks appeared beyond the river's mouth, and long before they reached the point took shape and became two barges. End on they came, heeling like one to the spanking breeze ; another half an hour would bring them to us.

The *Will Arding* was one of them, and we rowed off to her, and with a thrill watched her shoot up into the wind, while the mate let go her anchor. Three hours later she was berthed on the blocks.

The shipwrights nominally started work the next day, and I actually did so. I came by train in the mornings from Fleetwick and returned home in the evenings. The first job was to raise the limber boards and clean the barge out as far as we could reach, for hundreds of cargoes had driven their contributions of dust through the cracks in the flooring, and the dust, mixed with the bilge water, had formed a black ooze. It was one of the dirtiest jobs imaginable, and while it lasted my appearance as I went home in the evenings was so disreputable that often I was not recognized by acquaintances. An ardent Salvation Army man whom I met every day began to cast longing eyes on me.

After the cleaning, the *Will Arding* was tarred throughout inside, and then my thoughts turned to the cabin aft, for I sorely wanted a place where I could have my meals and keep my tools. Accordingly I cut a doorway in the bulkhead between the hold and the cabin.

In removing the late crew's bedding I came across an insect I had never seen before. Yet I knew what it was by the instinct that is said to guide men unerringly in those peculiar crises—like death—in which experience is wanting. *Nomen infandum!* To think that the creature dared to be in my ship! And then the dread assailed me that it was not likely to be the only one. Should we ever get rid of them? What would the Mate say? Had we spent all this money and trouble only to provide a breeding-ground for this horrible hemipterous tribe? I believe that I trembled. I was sick with disgust.

What I should have done, had I been a strict

A FLOATING HOME

Buddhist, I know not, but what I did was to burn sulphur candles, gut the cabin of every vestige of wood, and subject each piece removed to the flame of a blow-lamp, while repeating to myself a kind of fierce incantation : ' Let none of them escape me.' After that I squirted the whole place with a powerful disinfectant, then put on black varnish, then lime-wash over the black varnish, and as a final precaution I had the cabin sprayed with formaldehyde. As a matter of fact, the gutting must have destroyed everything, but I did not mean to take any risks.

When my peace of mind was restored, I proceeded to match-line the hold throughout.

All this time the shipwright, in spite of promises of the most binding order, was not getting on with his work. At the end of each week he would promise to put a hand on ' in the forepart of the week ' ; and at the beginning of each week he would promise again for ' the latter part of the week.' I kept chasing him and worrying him, and this distressing occupation seriously interfered with my own work. Moreover, it became increasingly difficult to find him, for he instructed a small boy on the quay to report my appearance on deck. I bought the boy off with sweets, and told the shipwright what I thought about him and his promises, while he scratched his head like an Oriental tranquilly contemplating the decrees of destiny.

A FLOATING HOME

The next move on the old man's part was to lend me an apprentice—this with the twofold object of keeping me quiet by rendering me help, and providing a messenger and intermediary who could be trusted never to find him. The old man's idea of business was never to refuse work, and to do enough of each job to make it impossible for a vessel to be taken away. For the rest he trusted to his excuses and his customers' short memories to set things right.

It ought to be said that his excuses were not ordinary excuses. He was always the victim, and never the master, of his own actions. He seemed to think that this inversion of the normal course of things had only to be stated to be perfectly satisfactory to his customers. On one occasion he doubled the decks of a yacht belonging to a neighbour of ours. When the work was done, the owner found a thicket of nails sticking out under the decks in his cabin. He indignantly asked for an explanation. The old man scratched his head and turned to his son.

'They was ordin'ry deck nails, warn't they, Tom ?'

'Yes, yes,' said Tom dutifully.

'But damn it all, look at my cabin !'

'They was ordin'ry deck nails,' the old man said again, and added, ' Well, to tell yaou the truth, sir, them blessed ould decks was too thin.'

At last I presented the shipwright with an ultimatum, to which he replied by putting a wheel-wright on to my work, and a worse workman in a ship I never came across. It was already six weeks after the date on which the *Will Arding* was to have been finished, and I now went on strike. The rest of the work, I decided, should be done at home eight miles farther up the river.

As ill luck would have it, it was blowing the better part of a gale the next day, the wind being on shore and a trifle down the river. In the yard it was said that the barge could not be moved. However, at that time I knew more about shipwrights' excuses and less about barges than I do now, and I insisted that she should go, whatever the weather.

' That ain't fit for she to goo,' the old man kept saying. He was right, but I was firm. And he, for his part, having spent his life in measuring human patience, knew when it was impossible to hold out any longer. So he gave orders for his men to get the *Will Arding* off the blocks. I cleared out of the way half a dozen dinghies, which she might foul as she came off.

It certainly was a wild day; the wind shrieked in the rigging, the waves curled and broke against the quay, the little boats close in shore pitched and jarred, throwing the spray from them, and the masts of the smacks and yachts in the anchorage waved jerkily against the racing sky. There was no time to be lost, for the barge had to be got off while the

A FLOATING HOME

tide was still flowing, or not at all. An ex-bargeman was in charge, and four hands helped on board. At the last moment it was found that a new mainsheet was wanted, and this delayed us, but we still had just enough time. The topsail slatted so fiercely as it was hoisted that it had to be half dropped again until the squall passed. The mainsail, half set, banged noisily and the mainsheet blocks lashed terrifically to and fro. As the foresail filled and the head paid off the anchor was broken out, and happily the barge quickly gathered way, for under her lee was a mass of small boats that I had not been able to move. Had she sagged appreciably to leeward she would have swept them all.

The start was a truly exhilarating affair, more like that of a young horse driven for the first time, and bolting down a crowded street, than of an experienced barge getting under way. The sails were only half set and slatting angrily; the running gear, from long disuse, was all over the place; one gaunt figure like a Viking, with blue eyes and long fair hair streaming in the wind, stood in the bows bawling which way to steer; another man amidships shouted the orders on to the helmsman; and thus, with two men at the wheel, the *Will Arding* with a foaming wake tore headlong through the small craft. She sailed right over one dinghy, but luckily did not hurt it. Several times my heart was in my mouth,

A FLOATING HOME

for in that packed anchorage we might have done enormous damage.

My tongue became less dry as the risks decreased, and never did the shout, ' Shove her raound !' fall with a more welcome sound on my ears than when, clear to windward of the anchored fleet, the *Will Arding* swung round on the other tack and stood up the empty river. I would not undertake that dash again to-day. One of the helmsmen remarked, ' I reckon that skeert some o' they little bo'ts to see us thriddlin' among 'em. That wind's suthen tetchy to-day t'ain't 'ardly safe, same as goin' as us did.'

At the end of the reach I dropped all my helpers, except one hand, who remained on board as watchman. As the tide had turned I anchored, was put on shore, and went home by train.

The next day the Mate and the hand and I brought the *Will Arding* up the rest of the way to Fleetwick and berthed her. She now lay within a short walk of our cottage. Labour, though not skilled carpenter's labour, was to be got easily enough. It would, at all events, be prompt and willing work. I had left professional assistance behind, but I felt nearly sure that we should make better progress at Fleetwick ; and I even ventured to think that the quality of our carpentering might not shame us after all.

CHAPTER VIII

'Ah ! what a wondrous thing it is
  To note how many wheels of toil
One thought, one word, can set in motion !
There's not a ship that sails the ocean,
  But every climate, every soil,
Must bring its tribute, great or small,
And help to build the wooden wall !'

IT was a curious thing that the greatest of the
advantages of living in a barge disclosed itself unexpectedly. When we made up our minds to buy a
barge I was free to live where I pleased, but shortly
after we had bought her I received an offer of an
appointment which would require me to be in
London every day. I could not afford to refuse
this appointment, and we reflected what a pretty
mess we should have been in if we had taken a
house in the town where we had intended to send
the boys to school. We should have had to get rid
of the lease of the house, and probably have lost a
good deal of money in the transaction. As it was, we
had only to withdraw the boys' names from the
school, choose another school within striking distance
of London, and anchor our barge fairly near a rail-

A FLOATING HOME

way station from which I could travel daily to London. The change of plan cost us nothing.

My work in London was to begin in September, but when I found it impossible to finish the barge in time, I applied for a month's postponement, and the partners in the firm, who were yachtsmen, admitted the propriety of my request and granted it like sportsmen.

The barge had now to be completed at breakneck speed. The haste robbed the entertaining labour of part of its joy ; still, we experienced a good deal of that satisfaction which is presumably enjoyed in primitive societies where every man builds his own house and goes hunting for his dinner.

We could bicycle from our cottage to the quay at Fleetwick in five minutes. I engaged to help me two handy men : Tom, a sailor, and Harry, a landsman, both, like myself, rough carpenters. Of course, everyone in the place came to see the *Will Arding;* never before had there been so many loiterers on the quay. People came on board so freely to watch the floating house daily grow into shape under our hands that I grew expert at mechanically repeating my explanations with nails in my mouth while I kept to my work.

The most keenly interested, as well as the most regular and most welcome of our visitors, was Sam Prawle, the ex-barge skipper already mentioned, who lived in a smack moored in the saltings. He made

A FLOATING HOME

his living by looking after a few small yachts. He came most days during the dinner-hour, studied what we were doing, and gave us his views. 'If more people knaowed what could be done with a little ould barge, less housen would be built,' he would say, with a shake of his head. He was always ready to discuss the advantages of living in a vessel. As a matter of fact, since the death of his wife, who used to take in lodgers, he had been unable to afford a house, but to hear him talk one would have thought that he had been taxed off the face of the land. And after his prolonged visit to the inn on Saturday, where he learned all his news—for he could not read—and had discussed the political situation and the infamy of the local rates, and had got everything in his head well mixed up, he would be decidedly 'agin the Government.' 'What I says is this,' he remarked once, in summarizing the appalling situation. 'We shall 'ave to 'ave suthen different to what we 'ave got, or else we shall 'ave to 'ave suthen else '—as illuminating a judgment as one commonly meets with in political discussions.

We worked up forward to begin with, because the main hold had in it about four thousand square feet of match-lining, two thousand square feet of three-ply wood, one thousand square feet of flooring, and half a mile of beadings of different sorts, besides the bath, kitchen range, and a hundred other things which took up room. We gradually got rid of stuff

A FLOATING HOME

from the hold as we worked our way aft. Within a few days the appearance of the *Will Arding* wonderfully changed. While we were still at Bridgend, the hold, the sides, coamings and bulkheads, had shown nothing but one great expanse of tarred surface, whereas now we had clean match-lining round the sides and on the forward bulkhead.

The total length of the barge is about seventy-four feet, and her beam is seventeen feet at the level of the deck and fifteen on the floor. At each end there is a bulkhead shutting off what used to be the forecastle forward and what used to be the skipper's cabin aft. The length between the bulkheads is fifty feet. The headroom under the decks varies from four feet three to five feet eight, and under the cabin tops, which measure respectively thirty feet by ten and ten by ten, the headroom is between seven feet three and nine feet. We made the cabin tops out of the hatches by nailing match-lining on them lengthwise and covering them with tarpaulin dressed with red ochre and oil. Thus we had two fine roofs, and these were raised on strong frames supported by stanchions bolted on to the coamings. Between the stanchions we fitted the windows. As the windows are high up and there are plenty of them, the interior of the vessel is very light and airy. The saloon is sixteen feet long by fourteen feet nine inches wide, and is, of course, the most important room.

A FLOATING HOME

As has been said, we began our work forward, and the first job was to divide the forecastle into a triangular sleeping cabin and a scullery of the same shape. Then we divided the space under the fore-cabin top and put up a partition, forming on one side a large cabin (the owner's cabin), and on the other a kitchen, a narrow passage, and a bathroom. The bath had to be put in position first, and the bath-room built round it, as there would have been no room to turn a bath in the narrow passage.

We have often wondered since what we should do if anything happened to the bath, for a consider-able part of the ship would have to be pulled to pieces to get it out. Perhaps we could have a rubber lining made for it ; but still it is a good solid porce-lain enamel bath, and ought to last as long as the ship.

The one space without light and with little headroom was abreast of the mast, and this naturally offered itself as the best place for the water-tanks. We could not afford to buy new water-tanks, so we went to a shipbreaker's, and were lucky enough to find two four hundred gallon tanks measuring four feet by four feet each, which just fitted in under the decks. At the same place we bought six mahogany ship's doors for £4, and these we scraped and varnished, so that they looked very handsome. The tanks had to be put in their places at a very early stage, as they were to be built in like the bath. Empty they

A FLOATING HOME

weighed about five hundredweight each, and were bulky things to handle. However, with tackles and guys and Sam Prawle's help, we got them through our furniture hatch and safely down into the hold, where we levered them into position, and wedged them in safely. The great size of our water-tanks was the only fault Sam ever found with the barge's internal arrangements, and his eye brightened sympathetically when I pointed out that if we found that they held more water than we wanted, one of them could always be filled with beer.

At the after end of the narrow passage already mentioned we made the dining-room, which opened aft into the saloon. Forward of the saloon on the starboard side came the spare cabin. Aft of the saloon on the same side was our daughter's cabin. On the port after side was a lobby with steps descending from the deck ; and aft of the lobby was the boys' cabin, which had been the skipper's cabin in the barge's trading days.

The rapid progress we seemed to make during the first few days at Fleetwick was in a way deceptive. It does not take long to put up partitions and hang doors. The result looks like cabins. Yet only the fringe of the work has then been touched. The finishing is the true labour. The underneath part of the rough tarred decks, for instance, had to be covered with three-ply wood, well sand-papered, before it could be painted and enamelled. The deck beams, worn and knocked about, had to be cased in ; nail holes had to be stopped with putty, and the joins all covered with beadings. Then there was the making of the cupboards and shelves and bunks. There was never a right angle ; we were always working to odd shapes. Indeed, there was so much to do that at times I was bewildered where to begin, and only by tackling the first job I saw, whether it strictly should have been the next or not, and putting Tom and Harry on to it too, could I regain a sense of performing effectual labour.

The wood bought in London was not much more than half what we ultimately used. Before we had finished we used over a mile of beading. Oppressed with the continual sense of working against time, my brain became so active that I slept badly. My life seemed to consist of sawing up miles of wood, and driving in millions of nails. I was pursued by dreams, after the manner of illustrated statistics in magazines, in which I saw black columns denoting the various amounts of material used, or tables showing how the material would reach from London to Birmingham, or pictures demonstrating that the nails in one scale would balance a motor omnibus in the other.

When the dining-cabin was nearly finished we gave a tea-party to celebrate the occasion, and while we were sitting round the table we saw through the windows the legs of a party of strangers.

A FLOATING HOME

The fame of the *Will Arding* had spread so far that people came on board who had not the most indirect of excuses for taking up my time. Being proud of the ship, however, and sympathetic towards all inquiring minds, particularly in nautical matters, I was glad to explain things to everybody. At least, I did so to all whose manners were passable. I developed a high power of curtness to the quite considerable class of people who seemed to think that it was my duty to provide a sort of free exhibition for which it was not even necessary to say 'Thank you.' Tom, for some not very good reason, regarded the arrival of strangers during our tea-party as a particular offence, and we heard him begin to parley with them on deck with : 'The guvnor says this is a 'alf-guinea day, and yaou can get the tickets at the Ship Inn.'

CHAPTER IX

'I reckon there's nawthen like sailormen's wit
To straighten a rop' what 'as got turns in it;
Ould Live Ashore Johnny 'ud pucker all day,
An' yit niver light on the sailorman's way !'

MEMORIES of those laborious days at Fleetwick Quay
are not only of carpentering, painting, and plumbing.
Sam Prawle provided an intermittent accompani-
ment of anecdote and observation which it is impossible to separate from the record of work done.
During the dinner-hour he would sometimes begin
and finish a considerable narrative. On the day when
we lowered our tanks into position he illustrated
his theme that people may put themselves to a
great deal of unnecessary trouble by telling us an
episode in the life of ' Ould Gladstone,' the white
mare at Wick House. Here is the yarn :

'I dare say yaou don't fare to remember ould
Gladstone at the Ferry Boat Inn down at Wick
House twenty year ago. Wonnerful little mare,
she were and lived to be thirty year ould, she
did. When ould Amos Staines sould the inn a
young feller from Lunnon bought it—a reg'lar

76

A FLOATING HOME

cockney, he were, and den't knaow nawthen about b'ots nor farmin' nor nawthen, and a course 'e 'ad to keep a man to work the ferry. What 'e come for I can't rightly say, 'cept he said 'e allus fancied keepin' a pub.

'The lies that young feller used to tell us chaps, same as fishermen, bargemen, and drudgermen what used the inn, abaout Lunnon was a fair masterpiece. Mighty clever he thought he were, and wonnerful fond o' thraowin' 'is weight abaout, which 'e den't knaow 'is own weight.

'Well, twenty year ago come next March, in the forepart o' the month, me and Jim and Lishe Appleby, the two brothers what 'ad the little ould *Viper*, 'ad a stroke of luck over a little salvage job with a yacht, and a course we spent a bit extry at the Ferry. Cockney Smith—leastways, that was what we allus called 'im—'eard all abaout our salvage job, and nearly got 'imself put in the river by the things what 'e said abaout it. Jim and Lishe 'ould 'ave done it, for they was wonnerful fond of a glass and a joke, as the sayin' is, but I 'ouldn't let 'em, cos I reckoned Cockney Smith might 'ave the law of 'em. A wonnerful disagreeable chap was Cockney Smith ; 'e used to read bits aout of newspapers abaout robberies and that, and then 'e'd say 'e supposed they was salvage jobs.

'Well, not long arterwards 'e 'ad a salvage job 'imself. Jim and Lishe hired ould Gladstone and

77

A FLOATING HOME

Cockney Smith's tumbril to go to a niece's weddin' at Northend. They come back abaout seven o'clock o' the evening, wonnerful and lively, and just where the road bends afore you come to the Ferry that was bangy and dark they some'ow got ould Gladstone and the tumbril in the crick. Yaou knaow the place I mean, sir—jist where the road runs alongside the crick on the top of the sea-wall. A course the place is as bare as my 'and, as the sayin' is, for there ain't no tree, nor hedge, nor fence, nor nawthen; but none the more for that, ould Gladstone 'ad bin that road for twenty year, and there ain't a mite a doubt but what she'd a brought they chaps back safe enough if they'd left she alone.

'But there yaou are, yaou knaow what them weddin's are, don't yer, sir? Well, there was ould Gladstone nearly up to her belly in mud, and she den't struggle, for the artful ould thing knaowed that, *do*, she'd sink deeper. The tumbril was nearly a top o' she, and Jim and Lishe was mud from head to foot—in their shore-goin' togs, too. They come along to the Ferry, and afore Cockney Smith opened 'is mouth ould Lishe says, "Look at here, landlord, what your damned ould mare's done to we. Spoilt our best clothes, she 'as!"

'"Where's my mare and cart?" says Cockney Smith.

'"Ould Gladstone's stuck in the crick and the tumbril's atop o' she," says Jim.

A FLOATING HOME

' "Do yaou mean to say you've left that pore animal there ?" says Cockney Smith.

' " Ould Gladstone's all right," says Lishe. "Naw-then can't hurt she where she is ; it's only just after low water." '

'Cockney Smith he were wonnerful angry. "What I want to know is 'ow did it 'appen, and whose fault is it ?" 'e says.

' " Well, it was this a-way," says Lishe. "Yaou see, we laowed we was at the corner, and Jim pulled 'is line, and ould Gladstone was a bit quick on the hellum, and afore we knaowed where we was we an' all was in the crick."

' " I've druv' ould Gladstone many a time this last eighteen year, and she ain't never answered 'er hellum that way afore," says Jim.

' " P'raps you 'adn't been to a niece's weddin'," says Cockney Smith, kind o' nasty like.

' " Ould Gladstone den't never git slewed in them days when she 'ad a proper owner, niece's weddin' or no niece's weddin'," says Lishe.

' " I suppose yaou keep pore ould Gladstone so short of wittles and drink that when she do git a chance she goes too far on the other tack," says Jim.

' " I've a good mind to 'ave the law of ye for spoiling my best togs," says Lishe.

' Cockney Smith seed it warn't no use a arguin', so 'e says, " Well, whose goin' to get Gladstone and the cart out ?"

79

A FLOATING HOME

' " We are," says Jim and Lishe—" that is, with some other chaps to 'elp, but this 'ere's a salvage job, this is," and with that they winks at Jacob Trent and Bill Morgan, two chaps off another smack, just to let them knaow they was in the job.

' " Salvage job be damned—robbery yaou mean," says Cockney Smith, and with that 'e goes off to look at pore ould Gladstone.

' We an' all went with 'im, but it was that dark us couldn't see ould Gladstone, but on'y the tumbril, but us heard she a breathin', so us knaowed she were alive.

' " Pore ould Gladstone ! that's a strain on 'er," sez ould Jacob Trent. 'E were wonnerful fond of ould Gladstone, was ould Jacob.

' When Cockney Smith got back, he were that angry 'e fared to be a goin' to bust, but Jim 'e says, " Naow look at here, ef ould Gladstone ain't got out o' that crick by half-past eleven she'll draown, for that's high water at midnight."

' " Yes, yes," says Lishe ; " and ef she don't draown she'll most likely get run daown, as the *Juliet Ann's* a comin' in this tide or next to load straw, and she's baound to stand in where ould Gladstone be with the wind this way."

' " Pore ould Gladstone ! that's a strain on 'er, that is, and she be wonnerful an' ould," says Jacob.

' Well, landlord he seed he'd lose ould Gladstone

ef he den't do suthen, so 'e says: " What do you chaps want for gettin' of she aout ?"

' "I reckon ould Gladstone and the tumbril's worth the best part of ten paounds, and one-third of that is four paounds or thereabaouts," says Lishe.

' " Well, I ain't a goin' to pay it," says Cockney Smith.

' "Then yaou can git she aout yerself," says Jim.

' " Yaou put she in, yaou ought to get she aout," says Cockney Smith.

' " She put herself in and spoilt our shore-goin' togs," says Jim.

' " Look at here, landlord," says Lishe. " Me and Jim 'on't say nawthen abaout our togs, and we an' all will spend half the four paounds here in drinks. We can't say fairer'n that, can we ?"

' That was getting late, so Cockney Smith agreed. So Jim an' all 'ad drinks, and then they pulled off and got warps and tackles and come and borried my ridin' light. As yaou knaow, sir, there ain't nawthen yaou can bend a warp to on that blessed ould wall, so a course they 'ad to pull off agin for a couple of anchors, and while the anchors was bein' got the others 'ad more drinks and waited for the chaps what was fetching the anchors to have theirs, too. Arter that they laid out them anchors on the weather side of the wall, and shoved some planks daown under the tumbril and 'auled that out pretty smart with a tackle on each side.

A FLOATING HOME

'When they come to start on ould Gladstone they was fair took aback to knaow rightly how to shift she, so they put the lanterns daown and 'ad a bit of an argyment. Bill reckoned she'd come off best the way she went on, but Jacob wanted to slew her 'ead raound so as she'd force her way off, cos she drawed most water aft. Jim said he den't want to think nawthen abaout that ; he knaowed they'd have to lift she with sheerlegs same as un-steppin' a mast. Lishe said they mustn't do nawthen in a hurry and must 'ave more drinks to talk it over, so back they went to the inn.

'Cockney Smith kęp' all on a tellin' of 'em to hurry, and the more 'e worrited 'em the more drinks they 'ad, and the slaower they was. First they tried Bill's way, and they wropped some sacks raound ould Gladstone's starn quarters to take the chafe. They only hove once, for poor ould Gladstone give a master great squeal, and when they slacked up she looked raound like as to say, "You fare to be enjoyin' yaourselves together, but I ain't."

'Arter that they bent a warp raound 'er ould neck and hove on that till they reckoned they'd most break suthen. Ould Gladstone struggled a bit, but that warn't no use, and then she seemed to kinder go faint and we an' all reckoned she was a dyin'.

'Bill said ould Gladstone ought to have some brandy, but Lishe said brandy were paltry stuff alongside o' rum, an' he reckoned rum 'ud pull she

82

A FLOATING HOME

raound best. So it were rum, and of course they den't never think to bring no bucket for ould Gladstone to drink aout of, so they had to use Lishe's sou'wester. Poor ould Gladstone den't seem to relish rum—leastways, she den't drink much of it. P'raps it was because Lishe had jist given his sou'wester a coat o' linseed oil. Anyway, what little she 'ad seemed to bring she raound a bit, and she opened her eyes, which showed she warn't dead yet. Jacob give she the rum because he served on a farm once, and knaowed abaout horses and that, and he was jist a goin' to pour the rum away when Bill stops him in the nick o' time. "Here, mates, we ain't a goin' to waste good rum what landlord has to pay for for poor ould Gladstone," he says, and with that he finishes it.

'Then Bill and Jim started to rig the sheerlegs, and Jacob and Lishe laid the planks to keep the legs from sinking in the mud, and while they were a doin' that Lishe fell off his plank stern first in the mud, and Jacob laughed till he nigh fell off his, too.

'Then Lishe went off to the Ferry to 'ave a clent up, and a course t'others followed, all a lingerin' for more drinks.

'I never seed a merrier crew than they an' all was when they mustered raound ould Gladstone again. Well, they got them sheerlegs rigged at last, but 'adn't got enough sacks to put under ould Gladstone's belly to keep the rops off 'er, so they went back to the Ferry 'an 'ad more drinks while two on 'em got an ould jib, cos they couldn't find no more sacks. That was gettin' late then—abaout ten o'clock, I reckon—and the tide was a comin' well up in the crick and landlord fared to be a goin' off 'is 'ead.

'Soon as they got back, they rigged the slings and hove ould Gladstone up, and put some boards under she for she to stand on, and then they laowered away. I reckon them boards was greasy or ould Gladstone was too weak to stand. Leastways, she fell off 'em, and Lishe and Bill laughed till they most cried.

'But the drink fared to take ould Jacob different, for he were wonnerful unhappy, he were, and kep' all on a sayin': "Pore ould Gladstone! that's a strain on 'er, that is. She 'on't go there no more." And when they come to try again ould Jacob made 'em wait while 'e mucked 'imself from 'ead to foot tryin' to put the sackin' more better so as to keep the chafe off ould Gladstone's sides.

'Then they hove ould Gladstone up agin, and thraowed a few 'andfuls o' sand on the greasy planks; but it warn't no use, and when they laowered she daown agin she just slipped off and fell on t'er side in the mud. Them chaps laughed till they shook like dawgs, all 'cept ould Jacob, and 'e jist kep' all on a sayin', "Pore ould Gladstone, pore ould Gladstone !"

84

MALDON

A FLOATING HOME

'Then Cockney Smith come along a spufflin' and a swearing abaout the time they chaps was takin'; and then they seed the tide come a sizzling 'igher up the crick, and that sobered 'em a bit, and Jim says, "We're on the wrong tack, mates; we must have them barrels what we used for floating *Hornet* t'other day and lash they daown taut under ould Gladstone's bilges."

'"She's a layin' on her side naow, so we can't get at she to do it," says Lishe.

'"Look at here, naow," says Bill; "if we lash them barrels together, we can heave ould Gladstone up and laower she daown on 'em."

'"I reckon that's the way," says Jim, "but them barrels must be made fast atop as well as underneath, else they might shift aft and float ould Gladstone's stern quarters up, and 'er ould head 'ud be under water."

'So they got them barrels and lashed them together, and laowered ould Gladstone on top of them and made all fast, so as they couldn't shift. They was jist a goin' back to the Ferry when Lishe says: "I reckon ould Gladstone ought to have a ridin' light up, so as if she got run daown the law 'ud be on our side, and we'd git paid all right."

'Bill said it warn't wanted, as they'd get the money as long as they got ould Gladstone out alive or dead. Cockney Smith said what 'e meant was 'e'd have to pay on'y if Gladstone come out alive, but 'e seed 'e might be alongside ould Gladstone if 'e said it agin, an' it warn't no use his arguin', as there was four agin him, and all three sheets in·the wind, as the sayin' is. Anyhow, Lishe would 'ave the ridin' light up, so he took and made that fast raound ould Gladstone's neck, and he an' all went back to the Ferry.

' They all reckoned the money was as good as in their pockets, and jist carried on anyhow. Bill told some wonnerful yarns abaout poor ould Gladstone when she were young, till they most fared to be goin' to cry. And pore ould Jacob 'e did cry, and sat there drinkin' 'is rum and wipin' 'is eyes and sayin', " Pore ould Gladstone ! that's a strain on 'er, that is. She 'on't go there no more."

' Cockney Smith he kep all on a dancing raound, tellin' 'em to go and look arter Gladstone, but Lishe, 'e jist says : " Look at here, young feller, ould Gladstone's all right ; she's got 'er light up, and if any craft run into she yaou can 'ave the law of 'er."

' We an' all was that merry—for a course they chaps stood we a tidy few drinks—that us den't take no notice o' nawthen. That must 'ave bin just abaout high water, and ould Lishe was a singin' a song which 'e stopped arter every verse to tell ould Jacob to kep quiet, when I 'eard a kind of a clatterin'. That bro't me up with a raound turn, for a course I knaowed at once ould Gladstone 'ad flet, and 'ad got aout o' the crick by 'erself, and afore I

A FLOATING HOME

could say a word there was 'er ould head a peakin' over the fence. We an' all run aout an' seed she a standin' there all lit up. That were the head master-piece that ever I did see. There she was, wrop up raound her neck and belly with sackin', Lishe's ridin' light 'angin' under 'er ould neck, and them casks under 'er ould belly, and the sheerlegs acrost 'er back, and fathoms and fathoms of tackle and warps towin' astern, and the ould thing mud from 'ead to foot.

' Ould Jacob and they an' all was makin' a wonnerful fuss over ould Gladstone when I come away aboard and turned in. Next mornin' I seed ould Gladstone lookin' a bit pingly, but not much the worse, standin' on the hard in the river and Cockney Smith a moppin' the mud off 'er.

' Not long arter that Cockney Smith sould the Ferry to Shad Offord, what's bin a sailorman and knaows haow to run a pub.'

CHAPTER X

' And around the bows and along the side
The heavy hammers and mallets plied,
Till after many a week, at length,
Wonderful for form and strength,
Sublime in its enormous bulk,
Loomed aloft the shadowy hulk !'

WHEN the match-lining was finished we covered
most of it with three-ply wood in panels. We
panelled the owner's cabin and the spare cabin
with birch. We made the spare cabin to serve also
as a drying-room, letting the back of the saloon fireplace into this cabin through the bulkhead. The
fireplace, a handsome brass yacht stove, was bought
second-hand from a yacht-breaker. Round the walls
of the dining-cabin we placed a dado of varnished
wood, and enamelled the cabin white everywhere
else except on the ceiling (our furniture hatch),
which we panelled. We panelled the saloon walls
and ceiling with oak, and enamelled the window-
frames and the uprights between them white.
Throughout the ship where there was no panelling
we put white enamel, making the whole interior

A FLOATING HOME

very light. In every available place we built cupboards and shelves; not an inch of space was wasted.

We arranged the bath like the baths in a liner. It is supplied with hot salt water, and the fresh water is used in a huge basin. The sea water is heated in a closed-in copper by a six-headed Primus oilstove, and a hot bath can be had in half an hour. From the copper, which is opposite the bathroom across the passage, the water is siphoned into the bath, and if the siphon be 'broken' it can be started again by the pump which empties the bath. Cold sea water from a tank on deck (when we are high and dry we must have this) is supplied to the bathroom by a hose which can be diverted to the copper when that has to be filled.

It may seem complicated, but it is not really, for the children understand the system perfectly, and thoroughly enjoy playing with the waterworks. Sam Prawle never grasped it, and bestowed on it his customary formula about any device he could not understand : 'That fare to me to be a kind of a patent.' It may be added here, in anticipation of events, that an appeal for help has sometimes reached us from a guest in the bathroom. On the first appeal the Skipper or the Mate goes to the rescue; but if a second appeal comes from the same person one of the children is sent as a protest on behalf of the simplicity of the waterworks.

A FLOATING HOME

The keelson is the backbone of the ship. Ours is about sixty-five feet long, roughly a foot square, and studded with boltheads. Right aft in the boys' cabin it is under the floor, but it is above the floor everywhere else. In the lobby it forms the bottom of the shelves; in the saloon it is covered with narrow polished maple planks; in the dining-cabin it becomes a seat; farther forward it is a platform for the copper; in the doorway into the owner's cabin it is a nuisance; in the kitchen it forms the bottom shelf for crockery; right forward it is useful as a seat under the forehatch or as a first step up to the hatch. In the saloon it is most useful to stand on for looking out of the windows.

We lost almost a day's work over a wedding. Harry's brother married the daughter of Mr. and Mrs. E. Pegrom. Mr. Pegrom, a platelayer on the line, asked me to give him a cheque in exchange for twenty-five shillings. And in the list of presents published in the local paper the twenty-five shillings duly appeared in the form of 'Mr. and Mrs. E. Pegrom : cheque.' In our part of the world a banking account is regarded as a sign of wealth and also as something mysterious requiring a high degree of financial intelligence for its management.

I tried hard one day to persuade Sam Prawle to open an account. I met him on his way to the post-office to buy a money order for six pounds to pay for varnish and paint. I pointed out that a cheque would cost a penny instead of sixpence, and was also a safer medium. I explained that keeping a banking account was perfectly simple, as all he had to do was to keep paying in cheques as he received them and paying out cheques to the people from whom he bought his goods, always keeping something in the bank. After describing the process several times, I asked him if he understood.

'Well, sir, that fare to me as haow that's like a water-breaker. Yaou keep a paourin' of the water in and a drawin' of it off agin.'

I thought I had gained my point, as he understood so well, and referred to the subject again a few days later.

'Well, yaou see, sir, I 'ave to work 'ard for my money, and I reckon a drawin' of cheques makes that too easy to git riddy of it agin.'

When the decks had been cleared and the lines rigged on the stanchions round the bulwarks and the outside of the window-frames painted, there was some outward and visible sign of the transformation that had taken place below. The Mate was satisfied that the lines would prevent all but exceptionally unnautical children from falling overboard; and as she was quick to assent to the proposition that our children were not unnautical, there were no further doubts about the matter.

During the discussion of this subject a friend told us of the engaging argument about lifelines which

A FLOATING HOME

had been addressed to him by a smack builder at
Leigh. He was having a small bawley yacht built
there, and when the finishing touches were being
put on her the builder asked whether the owner
would have lifelines on the bulwarks right forward.

'Yaou'd better 'ave 'em, sir.'

'No, I don't want them.'

'Now look at here, sir. Yaou 'ave 'em. All the
bawleys 'as 'em.'

'I know. It's all right for knocking about trawl-
ing, but this is a yacht.'

'Yes, yes, sir. I knaow she's a yacht. But what I
says is this : them lines 'as saved 'undreds of lives.
And if they was only a goin' to save *one* I'd 'ave
'em.'

We had now reached the stage of bringing
the furniture on board. I hired a tumbril, and with
Harry's help began the 'move.' The Mate and the
children went away for a few days to stay with
friends. I had to drive down seventeen tumbril
loads from the cottage, although we did not want
all our furniture for the barge. As there was
generally no room for me even to perch on the
tumbril when it was loaded, I walked a good many
miles in the course of moving.

A tumbril is a poor cart for such a job. The
jolting was excessive, and trotting meant ruin to the
cargo. When the back was up the cart held little,
and when it was down things were shed along

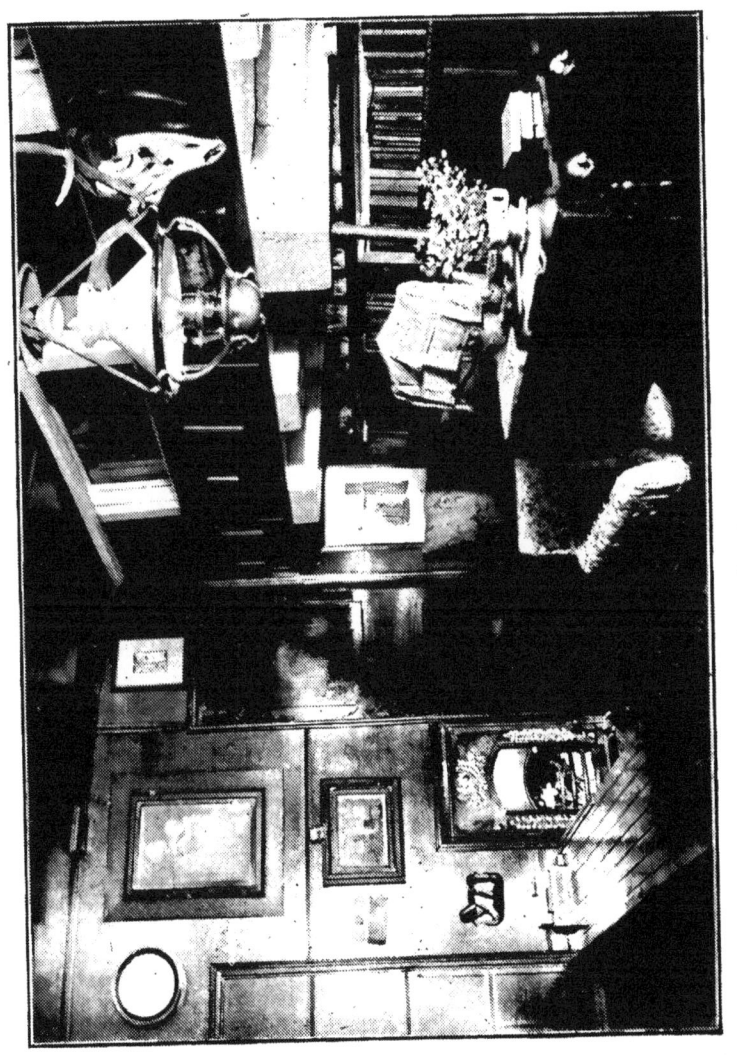

THE SALOON

the road. If I walked at the pony's head I could not keep an eye on things at the back, and if I walked behind the pony would slow down to a crawl. I partly solved the last difficulty by walking behind and throwing pebbles off the road at the pony.

At the end of the first day of this ignoble process of transportation I had enough things on board to be able to sleep there in comparative comfort. And at the end of the few days during which the Mate stayed away with the children I was able to tell myself that the barge at last looked like a home. The cabins were all furnished and habitable; the pictures were hung; even the china and books were arranged provisionally.

When for the first time I lit the fifty-candle-power lamp which hung from the ceiling of the saloon and looked down the long radiant room I said that I never wanted to live in a better place.

I cannot forget the pride of those first few evenings on board. Here was a dream come true. Wherever I cared to go my home would go with me and carry everything I owned; and the barge was not only my home, but my yacht and my motor-car. Every evening I held a kind of *levée* in the saloon. Tom had more sailor friends, and Harry more landsmen relations, than I had suspected. As for Sam Prawle, as critic-in-chief and privy councillor, he was licensed to bring on board as many people as he pleased. I learned that the race of bargees had all along known the best use to which a barge could be put, and I myself figured as a tardy practitioner in ideas which had been immemorially in their possession. Yet it gratified me to notice that they gaped a good deal at the transformed *Will Arding*, particularly at night, when candles as well as the lamp showered a thousand points of light on silver and glass and china.

Sam Prawle at one of my *levées* explained to the assembled guests that the simplest way of going to London was by barge. It was evident to him that I had done well to make myself independent of trains, which in his view were the confusion of all confusions. One of the most baffling experiences of his life, apparently, had been a journey by train from Fleetwick to Whitstable.

'That may be right enough for same as them what fare to understand these things,' he said, ' but I don't hould with them. Well, naow look at here, sir. When yaou get to Wickford ye've got to shift aout o' one train into t'other, ain't ye, sir? And there's two docks where them trains baound up to Lunnon berth. Five years ago we was in one dock, and year afore last it was t'other. Well, ye daon't knaow where ye are, sir, do ye? I niver knaow one of they blessed trains from another; that's the truth, that is; they all fare to me the spit o' one another. Then there's everyone a bustlin' abaout, and them

A FLOATING HOME

railway chaps a shaoutin' aout afore the train come, and when she do come most everyone's in such a hurry to git aboard that there ain't no time to ask, and ye don't knaow where ye are, sir.

'Then, happen yaou'll have to shift again half-way up to Lunnon, and happen not; that fare to be all accordin'. And same as when ye git to Lunnon, yaou've got to git acrost it, ain't ye, and when ye asks haow to do it, some on 'em says, "Yaou go under-ground," and some on 'em sez, "Yaou take a green bus with Wictoria writ on it." I ain't over and above quick at readin', and I daon't never fare to git as far as where she's a goin' to afore she gits under way. Last time I got someone from here to put me aboard and speak the conductor for me. But then agin, when ye git to t'other station and git your ticket, ye ain't found the blessed ould train, for that's a masterous great station full o' trains. No, sir, ye don't knaow where ye are, and that's the truth, that is. Then mebbe yaou've got to shift agin on the Whitstable line, same as I did time I went arter them oysters.

But same as goin' in a little ould barge or a smack with the wind the way it is naow. If ye muster an hour afore low water ye can take the last o' the ebb daown raound the Whitaker spit. Then ye just hauls yer wind and takes the flood up Swin till ye come to the West Burrows Gas Buoy. Accordin' to haow the tide is ye may have to make

95

a short hitch to wind'ard to make sure o' clearin'
that ould wreck on the upper part o' the sand.
Arter that ye can keep she a good full till ye find
the tail o' the Mouse Sand with yer lead ; then,
soon as ye git more water agin, bear away abaout
south an' by west and keep her head straight on
Whitstable. Ye knaow where ye are, sir, the whole
time, don't ye ? A course, if ye're a bit early on the
tide ye may have to keep away a bit to clear the
east end o' the Red Sand, but yaou must have come
wonnerful quick if there ain't water over the Oaze,
and Spaniard, and Gilman, and Columbine. That's
easy same as night-time, too, for when ye're clear
o' the Mouse Sand ye can go from the Gas Buoy
on the lower end of the Oaze across the Shiverin'
Sand to the Girdler Lightship that is, if yaou can't
go overland. Yes, yes ; that's much better ; ye knaow
where ye are the whole time, don't ye ?

'I ain't on'y took a barge above Lunnon once't,
and I remember that well, as I larned suthen I den't
know afore and that 'ad to do with trains, too. We
'ad just berthed at Twickenham with coals, and as I
'ad to goo to Lunnon to see the guvnor I goos off
to the railway station and buys a ticket, and says to
the fust porter I sees, " Whin's the next daown
train, mate ?"

' " In abaout twenty minutes," 'e says.

' So I slips acrost the road and was just in the
middle of my 'alf-pint when I 'ears a train comin',

A FLOATING HOME

so I peaks out o' the window and sees it come in from the westward. "That fare to be my train," I says to myself, and drinks my beer as quick as I can and goos acrost to the station again. But they shet the door just as I come in.

' " Where's that train a goin', mate ?" I says to the porter what I seed afore.

' " Lunnon," says 'e.

' " Yaou tould me there warn't no daown train for twenty minutes," I says.

' " No more there ain't," 'e says; " that's an up train."

' Well, that warn't no use a argyin' with he, and from what I could make of it that don't fare to matter whether folks lives above Lunnon or below ut. No one don't take no notice o' that, but allus says they is a goin' up to Lunnon.

' They Lunnoners allus reckon to knaow more'n we country folk, but us knaow better an that. Yes, yes; up on the flood, daown on the ebb; and that ain't a mite o' use tryin' to tell me different.'

CHAPTER XI

' O, to sail to sea in a ship !
  To leave this steady, unendurable land !
  To leave the tiresome sameness of the streets, the sidewalks and
      the houses ;
  To leave you, O you solid, motionless land, and, entering a ship,
  To sail, and sail, and sail !'

ONE day only was left to me, before the return
of the Mate, to examine the gear and make sure
that everything was ready for sea, as we proposed
to cruise for a few days before going to our new
quarters. The place we had chosen to live at was
Newcliff on the Thames, where there was a school
at which the boys' names had already been entered.

All the standing and running rigging and the
canvas were in good order ; nevertheless the waterside pundits had plenty of sagacious criticisms to
offer. Public attention was now diverted from the
interior to life above decks. In particular there
was not a new piece of rope or a new spar on
board that was not discussed till all its merits or
defects had been discovered or insinuated.

To a keen amateur seaman this reiteration is

A FLOATING HOME

never wearisome. He knows how to learn, because he knows that the most casual comment from a bargee or a smacksman is charged with experience. Many of these men have astonishing powers of memory and observation, powers as wonderful in their way as the sight and hearing of American Indians. Recognition of a vessel by the cut of her jib is easy enough, and has supplied our language with an idiom; but bargees and smacksmen will recognize one another's vessels at great distances, though even at close range the vessels may seem to other people to be indistinguishable. A few men can recognize any craft they have ever seen if they catch sight of only the peak of her sail. Barge skippers who have been in the trade a lifetime will recall the details of almost every voyage they have made—the time of starting, the shifts of wind, the margin of time by which they saved their tide, what they saw on the way, and a dozen other things—never confusing one passage with another.

When you sail by bargees or smacksmen at anchor you behold them apparently staring aimlessly on to the sea or into the sky; but they are watching. Perhaps they seem to be looking the other way, but they have marked you pass and noticed, it may be, that your topping lift is too taut. This or any other detail is duly entered in the unwritten log of their memories. On shore they take their leisure on the quay, walking up and down, never more than a few steps each way, with eyes always on the anchorage. The arrival of a stranger, the way he anchors, the coming and going of dinghies, the manner in which they are brought alongside—everything is noted.

Now, the chief object of interest in the gear of the *Will Arding* was a new kedge anchor. To men accustomed to anchor near the shore and in very narrow swatchways nothing is more important than their ground tackle. They spend more anxious thought on that than on anything else. My new anchor was lying on the quay, and I could hear the comments of every passer by. I was flattered by an accumulation of approval. Sometimes I was below, and did not know who was speaking; nor did it much matter, since the language of all was interchangeable. I would simply hear a voice; and soon another voice would be saying the same thing over again. Imagine a succession of observations like this:

First Voice : ' Yes, yes ; that's a good anchor, that is. As I was a sayin' to Jim this mornin', " That's got good flues, that has, and a good stock. I lay she 'on't never drag that," I says, " if that git aholt in good houldin' graound. No more she 'on't faoul that. That'll hould she in worse weather than what they'll ever want to be aout in," I says. " Then agin, that's a good anchor for layin' aout, for that ain't a heavy anchor to handle in a bo't," I says. " None the more for that, she 'on't never drag that.

A FLOATING HOME

The chap what made that anchor knaowd what he was abaout." '

Second Voice: ' That's a wonnerful good anchor, that is. That 'on't never drag that if they let that goo in good houldin' graoud. I allus did like an anchor long in the stock, same as that. Yes, yes; that'll hould she. That ain't a heavy anchor for same as layin' off in a bo't, whereas them heavy anchors is wonnerful ill convenient. Yes, yes ; they've got a good anchor there ; that was made at Leigh, that was, and wonnerful good anchors that smith allus did make.'

Third Voice: ' What do I think in it ? I don't want to think nawthen abaout that. I *knaow* that's a good anchor. She 'on't never drag that, *do*, that'll hev to be wonnerful poor houldin' graoud. That anchor's got good flues, that has, and she 'on't never drag that nit faoul it. They'll want to be in harbour time that anchor 'on't hould she. That's long in the stock, that is, but none the more for that that ain't a heavy anchor, and yaou can lay that aout in a bit of a sea when maybe a heavier un 'ould be too much for yer.'

The next day the Mate and the elder boy returned, and the barge was christened with a new name. *Will Arding*, no doubt, had had some sufficient meaning for the late owner, but for us it meant nothing, and we had decided to call the barge *Ark Royal*.

A FLOATING HOME

Before the christening we moved from the quay into midstream. The warps ashore were cast off, and the clank, clank, clank, of the windlass sounded like the music of other worlds calling. We slowly hove off the barge until her stern swung round and she rode free to the flood-tide and the east wind. Sam Prawle was on board, as I had engaged him to come for our first cruise in order that I might learn the handling of a barge under a good instructor. We could not start till high water, because the wind was up river.

Meanwhile, the christening was performed. Several smacksmen came off in their boats for the ceremony. A bottle of champagne, made fast to the jib topsail halyards, was flung well outboard, and came back on to the barge's bluff bows with a crash and an explosion of foam as the Mate said : ' In the name of all good luck I christen you *Ark Royal* !'

Everyone cheered ; other champagne (not the christening brand) was handed round, and we all drank success and long life and happiness to one another and the ship. The Royal Cruising Club burgee was hoisted to the truck and the Blue Ensign at the mizzen peak.

Sam stowed the wine-glasses in their racks below ; the good-byes were said ; the smackies clambered over the side, sorted themselves into the cluster of dinghies astern, and lay on their oars to watch the start. The tide was on the turn, the great topsail

THE *Ark Royal*

A FLOATING HOME

flacked in the wind, the brails were let go, and Sam and I sweated the mainsheet home and set the mizzen.

She was feeling the ebb now, and she sheered first one way and then the other, gently tugging at her anchor as we hoisted the foresail and made the bowline fast to port. Once more the clank, clank, of the windlass ; the short scope of the bower anchor came home sweetly, and the *Ark Royal* was free. I left Sam to get the anchor right up and flew aft to the wheel as she slowly gathered way.

We were off! Good-bye to the land and houses and rates and by-laws ! We believed that we were entering on a better way of life. We have since made sure of it.

I think of that first sail still. The newness to us of the *Ark Royal's* great size ; her height above the water ; the grand sweep she took as she came about ; the march from the wheel to the leeside to peer forward in bargee's style to see whether there was anything in our way to leeward; the size of the wheel itself, and the many turns wanted to put the helm down or up, filled us with importance and pride as we tacked down the river. If you would know what my feelings were then you must think of your first boundary to square leg, your first salmon, your first gun, your first stone wall with hounds running fast.

That night we anchored at the mouth of the

river, and when the sails were stowed and the
riding light had been hoisted, we ate our first dinner
on board and tucked our elder boy into his bunk for
the first time. Then beneath the stars, rocking
gently on a scarcely perceptible easterly swell, we
walked our decks in the flood-tide of happiness.

'None of our relations know where we are or where
we are going to,' said the Mate. ' Here we are now,
and to-morrow, perhaps, we shall get to Mersea Island
and pick up Margaret and Inky, and then we shall be
complete. Is it real ? Is it true ?'

We sat on deck very late, too much occupied
with the pleasure of existing to yield to sleep. The
sky was continually changing as snowy clouds
drifted across it. In the distance the Swin Middle
light flared up like a bonfire every fifteen seconds.
Here and there the lights of barges drooped tremu-
lous threads of gold on the water.

Sam Prawle was invited aft ; and regarding us
now as freemen of the barge profession, he enlarged
upon the advantages of barging (comparing it with
the sport of yachting, which he seemed to think we
had abandoned) with a confidential note in his voice
that we had not precisely detected before. But his
opinions on these weighty matters deserve a chapter
to themselves.

CHAPTER XII

SEATED on the after cabin-top near the wheel, Sam Prawle made known to us the *arcana* of barging. The comparison with yachting was to the disadvantage of yachting, and we felt that he would not have ventured to take this line had we still owned the *Playmate*. On the other hand, we were gratified at being treated with frankness as members of his profession.

'I don't reckon,' said Sam Prawle, 'there ain't nawthen as good as bargin', same as on the water, my meanin' is. Ye see, yaou gets home fairly frequent, yaou ain't got no long sea-passages to make, yaou can see a bit o' life in the taowns, and ef yaou've got a good little ould barge and freights is anyways good ye can make a tidy bit o' money.

'Then agin, in respect o' livin', most all barges carries a gun, and there's some I could name as carries oyster drudges; then there's a bit o' fishin' to

105

be done, and accordin' to where yaou're brought up there may be winkles, or mussels, or cockles, and, as I says, chance time a few oysters; so my meanin' is the livin' is good.

'A course that don't do for it to be knaown ye carries a drudge no more than that do to be seen pickin' up oysters nit winkles in some places, same as on the Corporation s graounds in the Maldon River. But outside them graounds that does no detriment. I dessay yaou remember some time back abaout they chaps what was caught pickin' up winkles in the Maldon River. Well, the judge give it agin them, for a course the Corporation has all the fishin' rights above them beacons. But the most amusingest part was, they chaps' lawyer tried to make aout a winkle warn't a fish, but a wild animal. Yes, yes; they lost right enough.

'Us allus used to live wonnerful well on the ould *Kate*, for I had a mate, Bill Summers, who was a masterpiece at shoot'n'. He were suthen strorng, he were, and had masterous great limbs on 'im, but none the more for that he were a wonnerful easy-spoken chap. I've knaowed he caught a many times by same as keepers and that, but he allus had some excuse or spoke 'em fair. Leastways, he den't never git into trouble.

'I remember one November day there'd bin a heavy dag in the fore part o' the day which cleared off towards the afternoon, and Bill went ashore

A FLOATING HOME

after a hare or whatever he could git daown on
they ould mashes away to the eastward there. A
wonnerful lonely place that is—no housen nor
nawthen but they great ould mashes. A course Bill
den't reckon there'd be anyone a lookin' after the
shootin' daown there, but there were. But as I was a
tellin' yer, Bill most allus knaowed what to say to
such as they. Well, just afore that come dark, about
flight time, I raowed the boat ashore to the edge o'
the mud on the lookaout for Bill. I waited some
time, and that grew darker and darker, and them
watery birds and curlew kep' all on a callin', and
one o' they ould frank-herons come a flappin' overhead, and that fared wonnerful an' lonesome.

'Well, I was jist a wonderin' whether I hadn't
better goo and look for Bill in case he'd got stuck
in one o' they fleets what run acrost mashes, or had
come to some hurt, for a man might lay aout there
days and weeks afore anyone might hap to find 'im.
Then I heard suthen and sees Bill a comin' suthen
fast along the top o' the sea-wall with another chap a
comin' arter 'im. "Ullo," I thinks, "Bill's in trouble,"
so I gives a whistle, and Bill answers and comes
straight on daown the mud towards the bo't with
his gun in one hand and an ould hare or suthen in
the other. When he gits half-way daown the mud
Bill turns raound to the chap a follerin' and says,
" Do yaou ever read the noospapers, mate ?"

'The chap, he den't say nawthen, so Bill stops

and 'as a look at 'is gun, and then he says agin werry slow, "Funny things you reads of 'appenin' in the noospapers."

'Well, that chap den't fare to come no further, and Bill finishes 'is walk daown the mud alone. Wonnerful easy-spoken chap, 'e was. Yes, yes; us allus had good livin' on the *Kate*.

'Then agin, same as summer-time, maybe yaou've got a fair freight, or yaou're doin' a bit o' cotcheling, and yaou're a layin' up some snug creek, and the tides ain't just right for gittin' away, and yaou has to wait three or faour days. Well, that's wonnerful comfortable, that is, specially ef there's a bit of a village handy. Or same as layin' wind-baound winter-time, maybe twenty barges all together—and I remember sixty-two layin' wind-baound at the mouth o' the Burnham River once't—well, that'll be a rum 'un if there ain't a bit o' jollification goin' on aboard some o' they. Yes, yes; I allus says bargin' is what ye likes to make it.

'What other craft can a man take his missus in—leastways, ef he has a mind to? They what ain't got little 'uns often takes their wives with 'em, and summer-time they can often manage without a mate in same as ninety-ton barges. A course, that's a bit awk'ard ef ye gits into trouble, for a woman can't do what a man can, and a man can't allus say what he wants to ef he has the missus with him.

'But that's true, women's wonnerful artful, and

A FLOATING HOME

I've knaowed a woman say suthen more better than what a man could. When ould Ted Wetherby—a wonnerful hard-swearin' man—took his missus with him, they was nearly run daown by a torpedo bo't in the Medway. That young lootenant in charge pitched into Ted suthen cruel, but Ted he den't say nawthen till that young chap was abaout in the middle of what 'e 'ad to say, and then 'e jist up and says, " Ush ! Ladies at the hellum !" And then the lootenant turns on Ted's missus, and tells she jist what he thought about Ted and the barge. Ted's missus den't say nawthen neither till they was jist sheerin' off, and then she says, " I don't take no more notus o' what yaou say than ef ye ain't never spoke." Bill tould me he reckoned that lootenant were more wild than ef Bill 'ad spoke hisself.

' Then agin, a skipper of a barge is most all the time his own master in a manner o' speakin'. A course, some says yachtin' is easier, and maybe it is, but I don't hould with it. I've met scores o' yacht skippers and had many a yarn along o' they, but I'd rather be skipper of a little ould barge than any yacht afloat. My cousin, Seth Smith, is skipper of a yacht, and he's tould me some o' the wrinkles o' yachtin'.

' From what I can 'ear of it, there's owners and owners. Accordin' to some, they what don't knaow nawthen fare to be the best kind to be with. Least-ways, that's a wonnerful thing haow long a yacht will lay off a place the skipper and crew likes. I remember one beautiful little wessel a layin' off the same blessed ould place week after week, so I ast a chap I knaowed if she den't never git under way. "Well,"'e says, " yaou see, the owner, he don't knaow nawthen, and the skipper and crew belongs 'ere. Chance time they do get under way, but we most allus says o' she 'ef there ain't enough wind to blaow a match aout there ain't enough wind for she to muster, and ef there's enough wind to blaow a match aout that's too much for she, as the sayin' is."

'But there's owners what sails their own wessels, and Seth says as haow they is good enough to be along with, for ef they gits into trouble they gits into trouble, and that ain't nawthen to do with the crew.

'But they owners what knaows a little is the worst, because they thinks they knaows everything, in a manner o' speakin', and the skipper has to be wonnerful careful. Yaou see, the trouble lays along o' the steerin'. A course, most anyone can steer, though they don't git the best aout of a wessel, but same as owners an' they allus fare to reckon that steerin' is everything, which a course it ain't. Seth has tould me a score o' times, he has, " Sam," he says, "that's a strain on a man, that is, for he's got to keep all on a watchin' his owner to see he keeps the wessel full or don't gybe she, or one thing an' another. Naow same as tackin' up this 'ere little

ould river," he says, " or standin' into shaoal water,
ye just says to me comfortable like, ' Shove the
ould gal round,' whereas my meanin' is that 'on't do
for a yacht skipper to say that to his owner. No, no ;
that 'on't do ; he's got to goo careful like. Maybe
he'll say, ' What do you think abaout comin' abaout
sir ?' Then maybe—if there ain't no visitors aboard
—the owner'll say, ' Let 'er come.' Then agin, maybe there's visitors aboard, and the owner 'e takes a
look raound and says, ' In another length,' or suthen
o' that."

' But ef the skipper's bearin' a hand with suthen,
or for one thing or another he leaves that a bit late,
so as he ain't got time to ask the owner what e'
thinks and let him have his look raound so that
fare as haow he's in charge, but jist says, " Shove her
round," quick like, then the owner ain't over and
above pleased—especially if there's visitors aboard,
as I was a sayin'. That's ill convenient, that is, for ef
she don't come raound quick enough she'll take the
graound, and then the skipper's got to say a hill has
graowed up or a landmark's bin cut daown or suthen,
and kaidge she off too ; and a course, same as on the
ebb, that's a hundred to one she 'on't shift till she
fleet next tide. Yes, yes ; a skipper's got to be
wonnerful forehanded as well as careful what 'e says.

' I remember a friend o' mine, Jem Selby, goin'
along of a gent who was wonnerful praoud o' his
cruises, what 'e did without a skipper. He on'y took

A FLOATING HOME

Jem, he said, cos Jem were a deep-water man and hadn't never been in a yacht afore, but on'y in same as barques and ships and wessels similar-same to that, and 'e wanted a man just to cook and put him ashore. Well, this gent and Jem brought the little yacht—I can't remember her name—from Lowestoft daown to Falmouth, and the gent was wonnerful praoud o' hisself, as they'd been aout in some tidy breezes. He was a tellin' of his friends at Falmouth all abaout his adventures, and the gales o' wind they had come through, when he turns to Jem, who was standin' by, and says, " What do yaou say to goin' raound Land's End to-morrer, Jem ?" " Well, I don't knaow, sir," says Jem ; " yaou see, we're a gettin' near the sea now." Maybe it were that, maybe it warn't, but 'e den't ast Jem to sail along o' he next season.

'Well, there yaou are now. Ye can't do nawthen and ye can't say nawthen. No, no ; from what I can 'ear of it and from what I can see of it, yachtin' ain't in the same street as bargin', as the sayin' is. Let alone, some o' they chaps never does a hand's turn o' work from one week to another 'cept maybe polish a bit o' brass work.

'Seth says as haow that ain't a bad job to be in charge of a little yacht with a party o' young chaps, same as on their holiday. Young chaps, same as they, never drinks without the skipper, and a course they most allus lives well, so the skipper do too. Then agin, yaou see they likes to do all the

A FLOATING HOME

work, and the skipper just puggles abaout like and tells they what to do, though a course they wants lookin' arter none the more for that. Maybe on dewy nights the skipper 'as to goo raound quiet like and ease up the halyards, for young chaps is all for havin' everything smart and taut ; but that ain't nawthen, and he can most allus do that while they has their supper.

'From what I see of it myself, I reckon young chaps same as they is a bit troublesome goin' into harbour. I remember seein' a party o' faour come into Lowestoft in a little yacht—a doddy little thing, she were—with an ould fellow in charge. The *Lord Nelson* was just startin' for Yarmouth, so they couldn't berth until she'd gone, and as I happed to be standin' by I made fast the lines the ould chap thraowed on the pier. Well, the band was a playin' and the pier crowded with gals a watchin' the yachts in the harbour, and they young chaps den't fare to be able to keep quiet like with them gals a lookin' on, and kep' all on worritin' the ould chap to knaow ef they hadn't better give a pull on this or a pull on t'other. Then I seed the artful ould chap give one on 'em the headrope to hould and another the starn rope—though they might just as well a bin made fast—and another he give a fender to, and t'other one, what was the most worritsome o' the lot, 'e took and made fast the jib sheets raound the bitts and tould he to pull on that. And he did. Lor', that did make me laugh suthen.

'Then agin, some o' they young 'uns hears things what they den't ought to. I remember young Abe Putwain, who used to sail along of a wonnerful larned ould gent what was always a lookin' at things he got out o' the water with one o' they microscopes —a master great thing that were, accord' to Abe. Well, this ould party and his friends was most allus argyin' abaout suthen, and a course Abe could hear they through the fo'c'sle door. Abe was the most reg'lar chapel man I ever knaowed, and used allus to hould the plate by the door every Sunday till he took up along this larned gent what I'm a talkin' abaout. Just abaout Christmas my mate left to take a skipper's job, so bein' at home I says to Abe, who I ain't seen for some bit, "Will you come, mate, along o' me, as yaour bo't's laid up?" So he come as mate, and one day, when we was sailing daown past the Naze and had just opened up Harwich Church, I says, "Well, mate, there's the ould church!" I says, meanin' the landmark. "Oh," 'e says, scornful like. "You don't 'ould with them idle superstitions, do yer?" he says. Well, that warn't no use argyin' with he, for he ain't never bin to chapel since, and that's what come o' yachtin', I reckon.'

CHAPTER XIII

'Here are our thoughts—voyagers' thoughts,
Here not the land, firm land, alone appears, may then by them be
said ;
The sky o'erarches here—we feel the undulating deck beneath
our feet,
We feel the long pulsation—ebb and flow of endless motion ;
The tones of unseen mystery—the vague and vast suggestions of
the briny world—the liquid-flowing syllables.'

THE riding light was already garish in the early
sunshine when we turned out the next morning.
The fragrance of the breeze coming in faint puffs
off the land, the clean taste of the air, the cries of
the sea birds, and the tender haze that overhung
the land, set all our senses tingling. Yet what a
creature is man ! As we stood by the main rigging
there came wafted aft to us from the forehatch the
bubbling sound and the smell of frying bacon, and
we could scarcely endure the delay of staying to
wash down the decks, though that was a duty to
be performed before hunger might be satisfied
honourably.

We got under way soon after breakfast, but the
wind was fluky and we drifted rather than sailed.

A FLOATING HOME

About low water we anchored in a clock calm to wait for the easterly breeze which we knew would come later, for the gossamers hung on the rigging. In the afternoon the wind duly 'shot up at east,' as the fishermen say, and we fetched over the Dengie flats, opened the Blackwater, and bore away for Mersea Island to pick up the other children.

We anchored in the Deeps, for there was no room for such a large vessel as ours in our old haunts up the creeks, but before the anchor was down two small figures in white came running down King's Hard. Inky and Margaret had been watching for us. We soon had the sailing dinghy going off for them. How pleased they were, how excited about their cabins, how astonished at finding their toys ready for them!

At last, then, our scheme was complete. The family was reassembled under a new roof, and that roof was a deck.

We met several sailing friends at West Mersea, and found our old yacht, the *Playmate*, from whose owners we heard an account of their first trip to Mersea. Off the entrance they hailed the man on board the watchboat, to ask the way into the quarters. The watchman, who had known the *Playmate* for years, and had seen her going in and out scores of times, answered the question in the spirit in which he supposed it had been asked.

A FLOATING HOME

He had not heard that the vessel had changed hands.

'Go on. *Yaou* knaow,' he shouted back.

'No, we don't,' bawled the new owners.

'Go on. *Yaou* knaow,' he repeated, as the *Playmate* forged on.

'No, we don't,' yelled the new owners, becoming nervous of running aground.

'Yaou let the ould girl goo herself, then. *She* knaow the way in !' was the last they heard.

During our short cruise we found out how best to arrange everything on board so as to avoid breakages in a sea. Our furniture, of course, had not been specially made for a ship ; some of it had already been screwed to the walls or bulkheads ; the rest of it could be quickly wedged. The shelves were all fitted with ledges, so that china and silver had only to be laid flat behind the ledges. On deck we hung thin boards over the windows, as these might easily be broken.

At Osea Island in the Blackwater we took in eight hundred gallons of water. We then visited Heybridge, Brightlingsea, and Wivenhoe, and still left ourselves ample time to make the passage to Newcliff and settle down comfortably before the boys were due at their school.

To revisit the Essex sea-marshes is always to discover something new. The dim low land may be called dreary compared with the more vivacious

A FLOATING HOME

Solent, but when the spell of this Dutch-like scenery has been laid on you it has touched your heart for ever.

Not all people who are in love with Essex have always been so. The charms of the county inland, as well as on the coast, have to be discovered gradually, because they are widely spread.

Essex has no cathedral which gathers up the interest to one point. Yet its houses are an epitome of its history and character ; they look as though they were part of the landscape, as though they had grown up with the trees. Some houses in Essex—farmhouses and inns—often welcome you with a clean white face, but the complexion of a whole village seen far off is nearly always red, and a thin spire generally tapers above the roofs. Churches and houses alike were built with the materials which were ready to hand. There is much timber in the building, because Essex has few quarries. In hundreds of churches, too, you may see the relics of the Roman occupation. The Roman bricks are worked into the lower parts of the walls ; flint commonly comes above the brick, and stout timbers are used not only for the roof, but in the whole construction. Sometimes the spire is made entirely of wood, and there is surely something beautiful and touching in the exaltation to this use of the characteristic material of the county. When a beam was wanted for a house, or a roof for a

church, chestnut was the wood, no doubt because
of the belief that no insect takes kindly to it. The
great building age of what is now rural Essex must
have come immediately after the suppression of the
monasteries, and you can hardly go into an Essex
village without finding a Tudor house. If it be a
manor-house, it may have a moat or a monkish
fishpond ; and perhaps the pigeon tower, which
dates from the times when the lord of the manor
had his rights of pigeonry, is still standing. The
old inns have a spaciousness which informs you of
the well-being of agricultural Essex when they were
built. Where the land is good there the inns are
good also ; where the land is poor the inns are
built on niggard lines. You can come across Essex
villages—such as the Rodings, the Lavers, and the
Easters—which for remoteness of air and unsophisti-
cation could not be matched except in counties so
distant from London as Cornwall and Cumberland.

Certainly Essex has no great hills, even as it has
no great buildings. But the value of hills is relative.
From many places in Essex only about sixty feet
above the sea there are wide views, and you may
gaze upon the Kentish coast thirty miles away
on the other side of the Thames. The secret of the
Essex coast is the illusion of immensity. The dome
of sky is scarcely interrupted by the small frettings
of land and wood along the edges. In this vast
atmospheric theatre a change of weather may be

seen at almost any point of the compass planning
its tactics on a clear hard line of horizon, and thence
swinging up the sky, showing the soft white flags of
peace or the threatening front of a battle formation.
One even has an important sense of the monstrous
nearness of natural forces when the 'inverted bowl'
is filled with a dark low-flying scud that seems to
be crushing down on you in a kind of personal
assault.

Men who have become captivated by the marshes
have been able to measure the gradual and unconscious change in their feelings about hills and
flat lands by a visit to some such spot as the Italian
Lakes. The beauty of the lakes has always to be
admitted—the purity of the water, the affluence of
the colour, the abrupt fall of the hills to the water,
the sweetness of the glinting villages perched high
up as though resting in a long and difficult climb
to the sky. But at the end of a week the visitor
may have found himself insisting on these beauties ;
he has felt that the sense of them is slipping away.
He who needs to argue with himself is losing
ground. He becomes unreasonably conscious that
the water is imprisoned, and does not lead to the
sea round the distant headland ; that the sky is
filched away ; and that the winds are false, being
misdirected by the hills and simply blowing up or
down a long corridor, so that Nature is frustrated
in these coddled and enchanted haunts.

A FLOATING HOME

In shallow estuaries like those of Essex the tides have necessarily to be studied more carefully than in deep waters. The ebb tide runs faster than the flood ; for the ebb is hurried seawards, pressed on its flanks as it goes, by the weight of water that pours off the flats from either side of the channel. The flood comes in from the sea like a cautious explorer. It is as though it could afford to be slow because it has the authority of the sea behind it. Moreover, it has nothing to do with the joy and madness of escape from confinement, but daily performs a sober function of renewal. It is a deliberate, sightless creature, pushing before it sinuous fingers with which it gropes its way through the crushed jungles of matted weed.

For the gulls, the redshanks, the stint, the herons, and the curlew, the important moments of the day are when the water first leaves the banks and a refreshed feeding-ground is once more laid bare. But to the yachtsman the vital time is when the sea advances, bringing its salt breath among the drowsier inland scents, raising the weed from the dead, and changing into sensitive buoyant things the smacks and yachts which have been stranded on their sides, heavy and immobile for hours.

There are two yachtsmen at least who are almost ashamed to confess how childish in its reality is their pleasure in watching the return of the tide over the flats or up some shallow creek. They have

A FLOATING HOME

not counted the number of times they have leaned over the side of a yacht, knowing she could not float for an hour or more, watching the tiny crabs scuttle into fresh territories as the oily flood bearing yellow flecks of tide-foam brims silently over one level on to the next ; watching each weed being lifted and supported by the water until its whole length waves and bends in the tide like a poplar in a breeze ; watching the angle at which the yacht has been lying correct itself until she sits upright in the mud ; watching, perhaps, in the proper season, the swish and flutter of the water, and the little puffs of disturbed mud drifting away like smoke, as mullet thresh their way through the entrancing green submarine avenues. And then there is always the thrill of the moment when the rising water touches with life the dead hull of a yacht, and turns her into a creature of sensitiveness and grace swaying to the run of the tide. One moment she is as a rock against which you might push unavailingly with all your might ; the next she has sidled off the ground, and will sheer this way and that in response to a finger laid upon the tiller.

As the tide rises towards its height you may see smacks—oyster dredgers, trawlers, shrimpers, and eel boats—filling the shining mouth of the estuary. The lighting of this part of the coast is like nothing else in England. A pearly radiance seems to strike upwards from the sea on to the underpart of the

A FLOATING HOME

clouds, which borrows an abnormal glow. In these waters, when the sea is not grey it is generally shallow green, and sometimes, when there are thunder-clouds with sunshine, it becomes an astonishing jade. At sunset the vapours over the marshes burn like a furnace, and the cumulus clouds sometimes glow underneath with the dusky fire of a Red Underwing moth. When the water has left the flats the lighting does not change appreciably, because the gleaming mud, glossy and shining like the skin of the porpoises which sport along the channels, has the quality of water. The most characteristic effect is the mirage, which swallows up the meeting-point of sea and sky in a liquid glare, exalts the humblest smack with the freeboard and towering rigging of a barque, and separates the tops of trees from visible connection with the land, so that they appear to be growing out of air and water. Often one might fancy that the trees of the Blackwater and the Crouch, thus seen in the distance, were the palm-trees of some Polynesian island.

On the marshes, or reclaimed lands, which are inside the sea-walls, and are intersected by tidal dykes called fleets, sea-fowl and woodland birds mingle : curlew with wood pigeons, plover with starlings, rooks and gulls, feeding harmoniously. Here and there the mast and brailed-up sail of a barge sticking out of grazing-land tell of a creek winding in from some hidden entrance, and remind you that in Essex agriculture and seamanship are on more intimate terms than are perhaps thought proper elsewhere.

Outside the sea-walls are salt marshes ('salts' or 'saltings') which are covered only by the higher tides. In the early summer the thrift colours them with pink and white, and later a purple carpet is spread by the sea lavender. The juicy glasswort (called 'samphire,' though it is not the samphire of Dover Cliff in 'Lear') changes from a brilliant green to scarlet. Herons wade in the rivulets; the whistle of the redshanks, the mournful cry of the curlew, and the scream of the gulls which fringe the edge of the water like the white crest of a breaking wave, sound from end to end of these marshes. In the winter you may hear the honking of Brent geese. But by far the most beautiful sight is hundreds of thousands of stint or dunlins on the wing together. These birds are also called ox-birds, and the fishermen call them simply 'little birds.' When they wheel, as at the word of command, the variations in their appearance are almost beyond belief; now they are wreathed smoke floating across the sky, and scarcely distinguishable from the long smudge that pours from the funnel of a steamer on the horizon; now the sun catches their white underparts, and they are a storm of driven snowflakes; now they present the razor edge of the wing, and then disappear in the glare as by magic;

BEAUMONT QUAY

A FLOATING HOME

again they turn the broadest extent of their wings, and a solid and heavy mass blackens the sky.

In May, when the sea-birds are hatching their young, the spring-tides are slack and do not cover the saltings. In a pretty figure of speech the fishermen call these tides the Bird Tides.

The lives of the fishermen are ruled by the tides. For them the working hours of the clock have no significance. On the first of the ebb, be it night or day, their work begins, and it is on the flood that they return to their homes. They have no leisure or liking for the time-devouring practice of sailing over a foul tide. The tide in the affairs of these men is absolute.

And although they do not confess in any recognizable phrase of lyrical sensation that the sea has cast a spell upon them, it is obvious that that is what has happened. On Sundays, when they are free from their labour, they will assemble on the hard—a firm strip of shingle laid upon the mud—and, with hands in pockets, gaze, through most of the hours of daylight, upon the sweeping tide and the minor movements of small boats and yachts with an air at once negligent and profound. The mightiness of the sea, like the mightiness of the mountain, draws mankind. Men have learned the secrets of these things in a way, and have turned them to their profit or amusement ; but the mastery is superficial, and it is man who in these great presences is unconsciously and spiritually enslaved.

CHAPTER XIV

'He was the mildest-mannered man
That ever scuttled ship or cut a throat.'

A GREAT merit of a barge as a house is that when she is 'light,' or almost 'light,' as the *Ark Royal* is, she can be sailed out of rough water on to a sand and left there, provided care be taken that she does not sit on her anchor. By the time there is only three feet of water the waves are very small, and thus, however strong the wind may be and however hard the sand, a barge will take the ground so gently that one can scarcely say when she touches. The explanation is simple enough, for, besides being flat-bottomed, a barge, owing to her length, strides many small waves at once.

We put the plan into operation on our way to Newcliff. We were running up Swin, and with the dark the breeze piped up; so instead of sailing all night or anchoring in the Swin, where there would have been a disagreeable sea on the flood-tide, we put the *Ark Royal* on the sand between the Maplin Lighthouse and the Ridge Buoy, and there she sat as steady as a town hall.

126

A FLOATING HOME

This is, of course, an easy way of going to the seaside, so to speak. You simply sail on to a nice clean sand and stay there till the wind moderates. Whenever the tide ebbs away, you can descend on to the sands by a ladder over the side, and pursue the usual seaside occupations of building docks and canals and forts and catching crabs.

It was a memorable experience, this passage up the Thames·estuary, house and furniture and family all moving together without any of the bother of packing up and catching trains, and counting heads and luggage at junctions. The children enjoyed every moment of it—the following sea and the dinghy plunging in our wake, the steamers bound out and in, the smacks lying to their nets with the gulls wheeling round them waiting for their food, the tugs towing sailing ships, the topsail schooners, the buoys, the lightships.

When we arrived at Newcliff we anchored off the town, intending to look for a good winter berth later in the year. After the quiet of Fleetwick, Newcliff struck us at once as over-full of noise and people. At all events, we had the satisfaction of knowing that we were not going to live on shore. The spot where we lay would have been well enough for the summer, though with a fresh breeze on shore it was impossible to take a boat safely alongside the stone wall. The boat, however, could be rowed up a creek half a mile away. Unfortunately,

A FLOATING HOME

this meant the chance of being drenched with spray, and it was also a too uncertain way of catching trains and trams. Nine times out of ten we could row to the stone wall, and when the tide ebbed away and the *Ark Royal* lay high and dry (which, roughly, was for six out of every twelve hours) we could always walk ashore. The sand was hard under about an inch of fine silt. Here and there it was intersected by shallow gullies, but short sea-boots served our purpose of getting on shore dry.

Of course, we always had to think ahead, for if one went ashore in the boat and took no sea-boots, it might be necessary on returning to walk to the *Ark Royal;* and if no one were on deck one might shout for sea-boots for a long time from the land before being heard. The most awkward time was when the flats were just covered with water, for then there was too much water round the *Ark Royal* for sea-boots and not enough to float a boat to the shore. Then one simply had to wait until it was possible to walk or row. Once we were caught in this way at one o'clock in the morning after going to a theatre in London. We waited a short time for the ebb, but were too sleepy to wait quite long enough. We put on our sea-boots; and then, slinging my evening shoes and the Mate's round my neck, and cramming my opera-hat well on to my head, I gave the Mate my arm. The water itself was not too deep, but in the dark it was difficult to avoid the gullies, and the Mate nearly spoiled her new frock and my evening clothes by stumbling into a hole and clutching at me. This was the only occasion on which I should have been distressed if those who had disputed the advantages of living in a barge could have seen us. In anything like a gale of wind there was a nasty, short, confused, broken sea, and then one had either to row up to the creek and be drenched or wait till the tide had ebbed. It was evident that lying off the town for the winter was out of the question.

Soon we found a berth up the creek where yachts are laid up, and agreed to pay a pound for the use of it for a year. It was well sheltered, but as only a big tide would give us water into it we had to wait some days after we had found it.

Meanwhile Sam Prawle, who had remained with us all this time, had to return home. The children had rallied him a good deal on his yarn about ‘Ould Gladstone’ and on the ethics of salvage generally. Salvage was Sam Prawle’s favourite subject; and we could never make up our minds whether he was more given to boasting of what he had done or to regretting what he had not done. The evening before he went away he was evidently concerned lest he should leave us with an impression that salvage operations were not invariably honourable if not heroic affairs. He therefore related to us the following episode, and the reader must judge how far it helps Sam Prawle's case:

' In them days, afore it was so easy to git leave to launch the lifeboats as that is now, we allus used to keep a lugger for same as salvage work. The last wessel as ever I went off to on a salvage job my share come to thirteen pound and a bit extra for bein' skipper, and if there hadn't bin a North Sea pilot aboard that ship us chaps 'ud have had double. But then agin, if us hadn't bin quick a makin' our bargain us shouldn't have had nawthen.

' One night, after a dirty thick day blaowin' the best part of a gale o' wind sou-westerly, the wind flew out nor-west, as that often do, and that come clear and hard, so as when that come dawn you could see for miles. Well, away to the south'ard, about six mile, we seed a wessel on the Sizewell Bank ; she was a layin' with her head best in towards the land. There was a big sea runnin', but there warn't much trouble in launching the lugger with the wind that way, though we shipped a tidy sea afore we cast off the haulin'-aout warp.

' We'd close-reefed the two lugs afore we launched the bo't, and it warn't long afore the fifteen of us what owned the lugger was a racin' off as hard as we dare. You see, we den't want no one to git in ahead of we. Us dursn't put her head straight for the ship, for the sea was all acrost with the shift o' wind, and us had to keep bearin' away and luffin' up.

A FLOATING HOME

You see, them seas was all untrue ; they was heapin'
up, and breakin' first one side, then t'other, same as
in the race raound Orfordness.

'As we drawed near the wessel, that fared to we
as haow she were to th' south'ard of the high part
of the sand, and that warn't long afore we knaowed
it, cos we got our landmarks what we fish by, for
we most knaows that sand, same as you do the back
o' your hand, as the sayin' is. We laowered our sails
and unshipped the masts and raounded to under the
wessel's quarter—a barquentine, she were, of about
nine hundred ton—and they thraowed us a line.
All her sails was stowed 'cept the fore laower torpsail,
which were blown to rags, and the sea was breakin'
over her port side pretty heavy. There warn't no
spars carried away, and there den't fare to be no other
damage, and if she was faithfully built she den't
ought to have come to a great deal o' hurt so fur.

'Then they thraowed us another line for me to
come aboard by, and we hauled our ould bo't up as
close as we durst for the backwash. I jumped as she
rose to a sea, but missed the mizzen riggin' and fell
agin the wessel's side ; them chaps hung on all right,
and the next sea washed me on top o' the rail
afore they could haul in the slack. That fair knocked
the wind aout o' me, and I reckon I was lucky I
den't break nawthen. I scrambled up, and found the
cap'n houldin' on to the rail to steady himself agin
the bumping o' the wessel.

A FLOATING HOME

'Well, she was paoundin' fairly heavy, but not so bad as other wessels I've bin aboard. Still, that's enough to scare the life aout of anyone what ain't never bin ashore on a sandbank in a blaow, and most owners don't give a cap'n a chance to do ut twice—nor pilots neither. I could see the cap'n fared wonnerful fidgety, for the wessel had been ashore for seven hours and more, so I starts to make a bargain with him for four hundred pound to get his ship off, when up comes a North Sea pilot what was aboard. I was most took aback to see him there.

'"What's all this?" he says.

'"Four hundred pound to get she off," I says.

'"Four hundred devils," he says.

'"No cure, no pay," I says.

'"No pay, you longshore shark!" he says.

'Of course, he was a tryin' to make out there warn't no danger to the wessel and nawthen to make a fuss about. You see, he was afeared there might be questions asked about it, and he might get into trouble. Anyway, it don't do a pilot no good to get a wessel ashore, even if that ain't his fault which it warn't this time, for the wessel was took aback by the shift o' wind and got agraound afore they could do anything with her.

'One thing I knaowed as soon as my foot touched them decks, and that was that she warn't going to be long afore she come off. Sizewell Bank's like

132

A FLOATING HOME

many another raound here; that's as hard as a road
on the ebb and all alive on the flood, and them as
knaows, same as we, can tell from the way a wessel
bumps what she's up to. I could feel she warn't
workin' in the sand no more, but was beginning to
fleet, and 'ud soon be paoundin' heavier than ever,
but 'ud be on the move each time a sea lifted she.
Howsomdever, I kep' my eyes on the cap'n, and I
could see he was skeered about his wessel, and 'ud
be suthen pleased to have she in deep water agin.

'"Cap'n," I says, "three hundred and fifty
pounds. No cure, no pay."

"Too much," says the cap'n, but I see he'd like
to pay it.

'"Too much?" says the pilot. "I should think
it is! The tide's a flowin', and she'll come off herself
soon; besides, if she don't we'll have a dozen tugs
and steamers by in two or three hours, and any of
'em glad to earn a fifty-pun' note for a pluck
off."

'"That'll be high water in two and a half hours,
and you'll be here another ebb if you ain't careful,"
I says to the cap'n, "and this sand's as hard as a
rock on the ebb. The pilot 'll tell you that if you
don't knaow that already for yourself."

'"There ain't no call to pay all that money,"
says the pilot. "She'll come off right enough."

'"Well," I says to the cap'n, "if I go off this
ship I ain't a comin' aboard agin 'cept for much

133

bigger money, and when she's started her garboards and 's making water you'll be sorry you refused a fair offer !"

' " I'll give yer two hundred," says the cap'n.

'That fared to me best to take it, for she was bumpin' heavier, and I laowed she'd begin to shift a bit soon. Then agin, the paounding was in our favour, for I see that skeered the cap'n wonnerful, so I starts a bluff on him.

' " That 'on't do, cap'n," I says. " I'm off."

' I went to the lee side of the poop, where our ould bo't was made fast, to have a look at my mates. The ould thing was tumblin' abaout suthen, for there was a heavy backwash off the ship's quarter. As she came up on a sea they caught sight o' me and started pullin' faces and shakin' their heads, and next time I see them they was doin' the same. I tumbled to it quick enough that they wanted to say suthen to me, and a course they couldn't shaout it out, so I threw 'em the fall o' the mizzen sheet, and me and one o' the crew pulled ould Somers aboard.

' " For 'eaven's sake," he says, close in my ear, " make a bargin quick ! She's a comin' off by herself ! We've got a lead on the graound, and she's moved twenty foot already."

' I went back to the cap'n, and he was all on fidgetin' worse'n ever, so I says, " Cap'n, my mates 'll be satisfied with three hundred paound."

A FLOATING HOME

' " Don't you do no such thing," says the pilot ; " she'll come off all right."

' " I'll stick to my two hundred," says the cap'n.

' I dursn't wait, so I closed on it, and the mate writ aout two agreements, one for the cap'n and t'other for me. Our chaps soon got the kedge anchor and a hundred fathoms o' warp into the lugger and laid that right aout astern, and I give the order for the lower main torpsail and upper fore torpsail to be set.

' Then our chaps come aboard, and what with heavin' her astern a bit every time she lifted to a sea and them two torpsails aback, she come off in half an hour.

' Yes, yes ; we got thirteen pound apiece, and if it hadn't been for that pilot we'd a got double.'

CHAPTER XV

'Mon Dieu, mon Dieu, la vie est là,
Simple et tranquille;
Cette paisible rumeur-là
Vient de la ville.'

WE engaged two men to help us up the creek,
which is narrow and was full of small boats difficult
for a large craft to avoid. Unluckily, there was no
wind, and we had to punt. This made our difficulties greater, as the *Ark Royal*, unlike her trading
sisters, could not cannon her way cheerfully up the
creek lest her stanchions should be carried away or
her cabin tops be damaged.

The two men used the poles forward while I
steered. A proud helmsman I was, knowing myself
the owner and skipper of the largest yacht on the
station, as we passed a quay thronged with long-
shoremen looking on. At that moment I had to put
the wheel hard over, and as the barge's stern swung
towards the land her rudder touched the hawser
of a smack moored at the shipyard. The pull of
a ninety‑ton vessel moving however slowly is
enormous. The hawser tautened like a bar of iron;

WALTON CREEK

A FLOATING HOME

the *Ark Royal's* rudder was banged amidships, wrenching the wheel from my hands ; one of the spokes caught my belt, hoisted me off my feet, swung me right over the top of the wheel, and dropped me on the other side of the deck. The Mate and the children did not seem to understand that this accident to the Skipper reflected some ridicule on the whole ship's company. They cackled with delight, and wanted me to do it again.

When we came abreast of our berth there was not enough water for us to go in, so we lay on a spit of sand and mud for that day. On the next tide, which was higher, we moved in stern first, leaving our anchor well out in the creek ready to haul us off in the spring.

The ebbing tide left us in a shallow dock about three feet deep into which the *Ark Royal* just fitted, so that with a ladder on to the saltings we could easily get on and off the ship. From the road, seventy or eighty yards away, there was a path across the saltings right up to us, but as it was very muddy we bought forty or fifty bushels of cockle-shells and spread them on it. We also made a bridge with planks over a small rill which cut across the path.

To the west of us was a sea-wall, and behind it marshes stretching away into dimness ; to the north was the railway line ; to the south, first saltings and then the open Thames. At high water we could see all the ships beyond the saltings ; at low water they were hidden from us. To the east there were gas-works, which we tried to forget, and the ancient end of the town with houses of many shapes and attitudes. One of the houses leaned over a quay against which smacks lay so close that you could have reeved their peak halyards from the top windows. There was only one house near by us, and in that lived a barge-owner, who welcomed us and lent us a broad teak ship's ladder. Such was the place in which we settled down for the winter.

As soon as we had driven in posts and laid out spare anchors, with long warps to hold us in position, we began to establish our communications with the shore. We found tradesmen anxious to call every day for orders. The postmaster promised three deliveries of our letters. I took a season ticket to London, as the time had arrived for me to begin my new work. The station was about eight minutes' walk from the *Ark Royal*. The boy's school could be reached in about twenty minutes by tram-car. We instructed the tradesmen's boys when they came on board to go forward and conduct their business through the forehatch. For visitors we hung the ship's bell in the mizzen rigging. I engaged a sailor-boy as handyman and crew.

The only thing that interrupted our traffic with the shore was the spring tides, which covered the saltings, for if Jack, the handyman, were not ready

A FLOATING HOME

with a boat, a tradesman's boy would have to shout until he was heard. Soon, however, the boys came to understand signals, and when a boat could not be sent at once they would leave the provisions on the grassy bank by the path, and someone from the barge fetched them as soon as possible. There were only about six days each fortnight on which the tides were high enough to make the use of a boat necessary.

Later we dismissed the boy, as a trusted family servant, Louisa, whom we had known for many years, came to live with us. As Louisa could not manage the boat, we set up a box on a post by the road in which tradesmen could leave our provisions.

If we had thought of the box sooner it would have saved us the robbery of a red sausage by a passing dog. The Mate and I were on deck, and saw the robbery committed. The time in which we launched the boat from the davits would have done credit to a lifeboat's crew. It was rather a long, stern chase after we had landed, and would have gone on much longer but for the dog's greed in stopping two or three times to begin his meal. As soon as we came near, off he went again, tearing over the grass between the saltings and the road with our flaming sausage in his mouth. It was a race between our endurance and his greed, and his greed won, for at last he lay down with the sausage between his paws and we fell on him from behind and captured

A FLOATING HOME

our own. The sausage had several dents in it, but it was not punctured. The dog had a good mouth.

As for mishaps to the food, more occurred on board when it was being actually delivered than when it was waiting on shore. Twice the milk-boy stumbled over the foreshore and spilt our milk on deck. A more serious matter was the butcher-boy's fall. He came up the ladder with his wooden tray on his shoulder one blustering day, was caught by a gust as he reached the top, and was blown backwards into the mud. Our joint lodged in the mud, and the wooden tray travelled a long way like a sledge on the slippery mud before it stopped.

Our coal was brought along the road in a cart, and man-handled from there to the fore end of the ship. We took only four hundredweight at a time, as we did not use much coal—the inside of a barge is very easily heated—and we did not care to have the decks hampered.

That winter, when an old barge was being broken up near by, we bought a large quantity of small blocks of wood to use instead of coal in the saloon. The coloured flames this wood gave off were delightful. As there was no room for the wood on deck, we built a platform on the ground alongside the *Ark Royal.* The platform sank a little, or perhaps it was never high enough ; at all events, when we had used only half our stock an enormous tide came, and the remainder of the wood floated

A FLOATING HOME

away. As soon as we saw that the tide was going to be abnormal we manned our boat and tried to salve as much of the wood as possible, but the tide rose too fast for us. First the blocks floated off in twos and threes, then in fives and tens, and at last in squadrons. We pursued them and half filled the boat, but a fresh westerly breeze scattered the Armada. We saw it spreading out and trailing down the creek as the tide turned. Nor was that all. Long before the blocks had reached the quay in their seaward flight they had been marked by eyes trained from childhood in the search for flotsam, jetsam, or salvage. Boats were launched, and our wood was picked up and carried off almost under our noses.

The annoyance of losing the wood was aggravated by the sootiness of the coal upon which we now had to fall back. Not only did soot lie about on deck in still weather, but the chimneys had to be swept once a week. Certainly this was a very easy job ; one had only to remove the upper parts of the chimneys on deck, hold them over the side, and run a mop through them ; then get someone inside the ship to hold some sacking below, and shove the mop down the lower parts of the chimneys.

Our supply of eight hundred gallons of water generally lasted about six weeks, for, as has been said already, we used chiefly salt water for the bath. To refill the tanks we could either move out of our

A FLOATING HOME

berth on a spring tide and take the water on board
through a hose from a neighbouring shed where
water was laid on, or we could have it carried on
board by hand. On the whole, we decided to have
the water carried on board, and our barge-owner
friend kindly allowed us to take the water from his
house.

As it did not much matter when the water was
brought, or whether the carrier worked one hour
or eight hours a day, we gave the appointment of
water-carrier to a hairless, red-faced boy of twenty
who lived in an old boat. As a matter of fact, he
was a man of about thirty-five, of whom it was
said by some that he was half-witted, by others that
he was lazy, and by others that he was artful. Anyhow, he suited us very well, for in the circumstances
he could not easily have suited us badly. He came
when he felt inclined, and with a yoke and two
three-gallon pails patiently, and at his own pace,
fetched the water, emptied it into our tanks, and
went for more. He generally made five round trips
in an hour, thus bringing thirty gallons. He never
worked more than six hours a day, at which rate
he could fill our tanks in about five days ; but he
generally preferred to spread the work over ten days.

Even where we lay beyond the town the *Ark
Royal* was an object of intense curiosity. Had we
made a charge for showing people over her, we
should have collected enough money to buy a
new mainsail. Among the strangers who became

142

acquainted with her internal beauties the most
enterprising and the most bewildered was a school-
attendance officer. He called one Saturday afternoon,
and was told we should not be back till the evening.
We were waiting for dinner when Louisa announced
that he had returned. We invited him to the saloon
and inquired his business. He had heard that we
had three children, and he had come to assure himself that they were being educated. Oh, the boys
were at Mr. Jones's, and were going on to Hailey-
bury? Quite so. He was sorry to have troubled us.
Then he, too, was shown round the ship, so that
we trust he did not consider his visit wholly wasted.

Although our berth was more than a hundred
yards from the railway, the trains—particularly the
expresses—shook the ground on which the *Ark
Royal* sat. At first the noise disturbed us, but soon
we became unconscious of it. For other reasons I
was grateful to the railway for being where it was.
On dark winter nights, when I was returning from
London, it never failed to please me to look out of
the train and see the warm radiance from the *Ark
Royal* striking up into the blackness. Then the
walk from the station along the narrow old street
paved with cobbles was delightful, and I could not
hurry because I must stop to watch an anchor or a
trawlhead being forged in the blacksmith's, or to
look at the mops, buckets, oilskins, sou'-westers,
compasses, foghorns, lamps, and tins of paint, in the
marine stores. And particularly at high water—if

the wind were on shore—as I came abreast of the openings between the houses I was drawn by the splashing of the waves against the quay. There I would peer at the dark forms of dinghies scuffling in the small ' sissing ' waves (as they say in Essex), or watch a cockle-boat with ghostly sails come racing home, and listen for the click of her patent blocks as she lowered her long gaff in readiness to berth by the sheds farther up the creek near the *Ark Royal.* I knew that unless I hurried she would be there before me, but then on the wide piece of quay facing the Flag Inn knots of fishermen would be pacing backwards and forwards, and civility or interest required that the time of night should be passed with them. Just then, perhaps, a green light close in would attract me, and forthwith the dark canvas of abarge towering above it would loom in sight. The short stiff walk of the fishermen would cease ; all eyes would strain into the darkness, and a discussion as to which barge she was and for what quay she was bound would begin. At last the barge would settle the matter by becoming recognizable beyond dispute. We would watch the great mainsail grow smaller and smaller as it was brailed up, and wait for the mainsail and topsail to come down with a run. Then when the vessel seemed to be advancing right on to us there would be a splash and the sound of cable rattling out, and her stern would swing round towards the quay and she was anchored. A dark figure in a boat, glimpses of a line, a shout,

A FLOATING HOME

'All fast!' the sound of more cable being paid out, and the barge's bows would swing slowly in towards the quay and she was berthed. Then the fishermen in their sea-boots, and guernseys, and billycock hats, or jumpers and peaked caps, would resume their stiff short walk, and I was free to go on my homeward way.

With sailormen it seems as though they felt that the safety of a ship while being berthed depended on their not taking their eyes off her. But perhaps they have no thought of rendering telepathic aid; it may be that they are only hypnotized, like me.

A little farther along the road one came into the open and could see the shafts of light from the *Ark Royal*. On dark nights the sailing directions to find our private path were very simple: go along the road until all light is obscured on the port side and begins to show on the starboard side; then you are abreast of the path. The richest moments of pleasure came when it was high water at night, and one could look over the saltings on to the business of the great river. Especially on Fridays and Saturdays large liners were bound out or in; there were always the clustered illuminations of the shore to the east and south-east, the avenue of lights on the pier, and the Nore flaring up and dying down; to the south the searchlights of Sheerness; and to the south of west the River Middle gas-buoys blinking industriously in the dark and guiding the sailor safely up to London.

CHAPTER XVI

'Mon cœur, comme un oiseau, voltigeait tout joyeux
   Et planait librement à l'entour des cordages ;
   Le navire roulait sous un ciel sans nuages
   Comme un ange enivré du soleil radieux.'

ON Saturdays, when I was always at home, there was plenty to be done. The mainsail, which we had not unbent, had to be aired and the blocks had to be overhauled ; and there were arrears of carpentering which never seemed to be overtaken. At spring tides we used to sail about the creek in the dinghy. In their holidays the boys made and sailed model boats and invented ingenious and daring swinging games on board with the falls of the halyards. And of course they invited all their friends to see our floating home.

We spent Christmas on board in great jollity. That time was marked by one mishap, though it presented itself to the children as an entertainment appropriate to the season. The *Ark Royal* during spring tides and a westerly gale blew partly out of her dock. As I was walking back from the station one evening something about her struck me as queer, though I

146

A FLOATING HOME

was some way off and looking at her broadside on. When I came nearer I could see that she was listing over at a very steep angle.

The children were frankly delighted, and told me incoherently and all at once how their tea-things had slid off the table until books had been put under the legs, and how the saloon door would not shut and the kitchen door would not open.

After unhanging the doors and planing pieces off them, we were able to make shift all right till midnight, when the barge floated and I hove her back into her berth.

The wringing of the barge on this occasion led me to try definitely to solve the problem of keeping her decks, and particularly the joins between the decks and the coamings, perfectly watertight. It has been already mentioned that all barges, owing to their length and build, alter their shapes or 'wring' slightly according to the ground on which they lie. On this account, if I were to convert another barge, I should hang the doors at once with a certain margin. All our doors have been unhung and planed two or three times. The wringing throws an enormous strain on the coamings, tending to pull them apart from the decks. You may caulk the joins thoroughly with oakum and serve them with marine glue, but a fresh strain will pull them open again. At last I invented a successful method. A quarter-round beading was fastened along the decks about a quarter of an inch from the coaming, and a hot mixture of marine glue and Stockholm tar was poured in between the beading and the coaming. The Stockholm tar gives the marine glue a permanent softness. We then covered the mixture with another mixture of putty and varnish, which protected it from heat, cold, and wet. The secret, in fine, is to caulk the joins with something that will expand and contract like the surrounding material without becoming detached from it. This something must remain soft and sticky. But if the mixture be not buried under something else it will melt and trickle across the decks like heavy treacle.

The decks themselves were less difficult to keep tight ; nevertheless, we had some trouble at first. We began by painting or dressing them, but later we covered them with a buff linoleum, which will be cheaper in the long run. The puzzle was how to lay the linoleum on worn decks. There were edges and knots which would soon have worked through. However, we solved this problem, too. We spread half a hundredweight of hot pitch, mixed with some tar, on the decks, and laid tarred felt upon it. Above the felt we laid the linoleum, with more pitch and tar to stick it. When in the mournful order of things the *Ark Royal* comes to her end, and is sawed up, burned, or ground to pieces by the sea, that linoleum will perish as an integral part of the decks, for nothing will ever separate them.

A FLOATING HOME

The winter passed, and with the swelling of the
buds and the gift of song to the birds our corner of
the world woke, too, and the yachts in the saltings
began to renew their plumage. On all sides were
heard the sounds of scraping ; masts and spars and
blocks sloughed their dull winter skins and glistened
with new varnish in the sun.

The *Ark Royal* also was fitted out. The whole
ship smelt of varnish and new rope ; the headsails,
topsail, and mizzen were bent, and she was ready to
move out of winter quarters.

On Maundy Thursday we cast off the warps on
shore, took our spare anchors on board, and waited
for the tide. I had engaged a sailor-boy as crew, and
also had a friend to help me. After five months'
silence we heard once more the exciting clank of
the windlass as we hove in the muddy chain. The
chain came easily at first, and then checked at the
strain of breaking out the great bower anchor from
the bed which it had made for itself in the sand. A
little humouring, and away it came and up went
our spreading red topsail. A fresh wind off the land
carried us slowly out of the creek through the small
fry. Clear of the creek we let the brails go, and the
wind crashed out the mainsail. Up went the bellying
foresail and then the white jib topsail, and the *Ark
Royal* was snoring through the water alive from
truck to keel. The great sprit scrooping against the
mast spoke of freedom after prison ; the wind

harped in the rigging; the rudder wriggled and kicked in the following seas, sending a thrill of pleasure through the helmsman. Even the dinghy seemed like a high-spirited animal that had been kept too long in the stable. She would drop astern with her head slightly sideways, and then leap and charge forwards at the tug of the painter. It was a translucent morning. The fleet of bawleys was getting under way, a topsail schooner was anchoring off the pier, a cruiser was coming out of Sheerness, a barque in tow was going up Sea Reach, there were red-sailed barges everywhere, and we were embracing 'our golden uncontrolled enfranchisement.'

'Where are we going to?' was asked several times before we reached the Nore. The point was that I did not know. So long as might be I did not want to know, for there is a peculiarly satisfying pleasure in playing with the sense of uncontrolled enfranchisement.

At length it became necessary to decide. Meynell suggested Harwich; Margaret, West Mersea; and Inky, Fambridge. But as we had no time to go so far as any of these, I asked them to choose a place in Kent.

Kent was a new land to them, and when I mentioned the probability of seeing aeroplanes on Sheppey Island they were all for Kent. So we headed

LANDERMERE

A FLOATING HOME

for Warden Point, and the fair wind and tide soon took us there ; then hauling our wind we reached along the beautiful shelly shore to Shellness and let go our anchor well inside the Swale about six o'clock. On Good Friday morning, taking the young flood, we beat up to Harty Ferry, anchored, and went to church. Most of Saturday morning we lay on a hill watching the aeroplanes tear along the ground, rise, fly round, and settle again ; and in the afternoon we sailed in the dinghy up to Sitting-bourne and bought provisions. All Sunday the glass fell, and towards evening the rain set in with the wind south-east, and on Monday it blew such a gale that a return to Newcliff was out of the question.

On Tuesday I was obliged to go to London, and as it was blowing too hard for the dinghy to take me to the Sittingbourne side I had to hire the ferry-boat. The two men who pulled me across were nearly played out before they landed me. Luckily my friend was able to remain on board the *Ark Royal* and look after things with the paid hand while I was away.

I rejoined the ship on Friday evening, and the next day in a fresh wind we sailed to Queenborough. We anchored near the swing bridge, and my friend went off in the boat to tell the men to swing the bridge for us. The bridgeman flatly refused, because, he said, the *Ark Royal* was a barge and could lower her mast. I then went to see the man myself, and asked him to look at our cabin-top and explain how the mast could be lowered. He admitted that it could not be done. As a matter of fact, it could have been done by taking off the furniture hatch and removing the upper part of the coamings, and spending the best part of a day over the job. But it was not my business to tell him that. Even then he seemed doubtful, so I suggested telephoning to Sheerness for instructions. He kept on repeating that the *Ark Royal* was a barge, and that he was not allowed to swing the bridge for barges.

Now I played my best card. I had brought my ship's papers with me, and producing my Admiralty warrant to fly the Blue Ensign and one or two other imposing documents, I hinted that further delay would compel me to report the matter. I noticed that he wavered. Then, placing a shilling in his hand and begging him not to ruin a promising career, I left him standing by the levers ready to open the bridge.

For the passage through we took on one of the hufflers,* and we anchored on the other side, as wind and tide were against us for the next reach. While we were at anchor many barges shot the bridge, which had been closed directly we had passed

* See footnote on page 24.

A FLOATING HOME

through. It is one of the prettiest sights in the world to see them do it. As the barges' topsails became visible over the sea-walls far off the hufflers recognized their clients and rowed off to meet them. The hufflers, the most curious brotherhood of all irregular pilots, live here in old hulks or built-up boats on the foreshore. The wind was straight across the river and fresh, and a barge would come tearing along towards the bridge with everything set. When she was quite close to the bridge—sometimes not a length away—down went everything, all standing, till the great sprit rested on deck ; and then, with her mainsail trailing in the water and a perfect tangle of ropes and gear everywhere, the barge would shoot under the bridge. On the other side she would anchor to hoist her gear again ; but if the conditions had been right she would have hoisted her gear under way and gone straight on. To witness the consummate skill of this feat is to respect the race of bargees for ever. Think of it ! The gear aloft—mast, topmast, and sails—weigh about three and a half tons, and there are just three men—one nearly always at the wheel—to lower and hoist everything. There have been many accidents and still more narrow escapes, for, besides skill and nerve, foresight is required to see that everything on board is clear. At Rochester there are three bridges close together, and every day dozens of

barges shoot them. It is well worth the return fare
from London to watch the performance.

The next day we returned to Newcliff, moored
off the town a little way outside the creek in which
we had spent the winter, and resumed our familiar
life.

CHAPTER XVII

'Get up, get up; for shame! the blooming morn
Upon her wings presents the god unshorn.
See how Aurora throws her fair
Fresh-quilted colours through the air;
Get up, sweet slug-a-bed, and see
The dew bespangling herb and tree.'

THE coming of warm weather and long days proved
to us that public interest in our floating home had
not dwindled. We were a good deal disturbed by
parties rowing round us the whole time we were
afloat; and even when the tide had left us, sight-
seers in pathetically unsuitable boots would walk
across the film of slime from the shore to look at
us. In Newcliff we had evidently become a legend.
Boatmen in charge of pleasure-boats would generally
head for us; and as we sat on deck we often formed
part of the audience as the boatmen delivered their
peculiar versions of the details of our lives. But
night would come and sweep away every annoyance; then boats were in the occupation only of
professionals and yachtsmen, who would glide past
us without stopping; landward noises were hushed,
and the land itself was seen but dimly against the

faint northern light thrown up from the hidden midsummer sun.

Sometimes we came on deck to see the dawn ; then we always felt ashamed that we had not more often watched that pageant. Men, indeed, know little of the dawn; there must be many persons of eighty who have not looked upon it more than a dozen times. And dawn at the mouth of a great river, or, indeed, anywhere on salt water, differs from dawn on the land, for the sailor, having to work the tides, will be off with the first streak of light, if the tide serves then.

One morning one of our anchors had to be shifted at daylight lest the ship should sit on it, and the Mate and I were present at the birth of a wonderful day. There was silence, save for the slight crepitation of the water being drawn between the leeboards and the hull of the *Ark Royal*. The east was the grey of doves ; the land was sunk in mist; then the mist began sliding away, and hills and houses grew by an imperceptible process out of the opaqueness like a photograph developing on a film. Seawards, the ruby lantern on the pierhead and the flaring Nore paled, pink wisps of cloud flooded across the sky, and the riding lights and buoy lights shrank to pin-points.

The Nore ceased to revolve, the shore lights guttered out, and indubitable daylight—how it had come one even then did not understand—fell upon

A FLOATING HOME

a fleet of long-gaffed bawleys mustering in the
Ray, and on a string of barges from the Medway,
spreading like a skein of geese along the Blyth sand.
Half-way between the retreating mists of the two
shores there lay a long black plume of smoke from
a steamer, and the drumming of her propeller
seemed to rise out of the water at our feet.

The day that followed was worthy of that dawn.
The sky was without a cloud, and the mirage
shivered on the water from shore to shore. Faint
breezes off the land yielded before noon to a clock
calm ; then flaws of air from the eastward smeared
the glassy surface; the cat's-paws became dimples,
and the dimples tiny waves, and at last the crests of
the waves began to break prettily and playfully
without malice. This sea breeze blew true and
warm all the afternoon, and when it met the ebb
the tideway was all sparkling till the evening. Later
the land breeze came again, and blew fainter and
fainter until it ceased, and

> 'The sun,
> Closing his benediction,
> Sinks, and the darkening air
> Thrills with a sense of the triumphing night—
> Night with her train of stars
> And her great gift of sleep.'

A particular pleasure of ours was to see the
fishermen return. First the fleet of bawleys would
anchor in the Ray a mile away, and as soon as the
sails were stowed the men would put their catch

in the boats to sail home to the creek. Two or three boats, perhaps, would detach themselves before the others like early ice-floes breaking away from the pack. Then groups would shove away from the fleet and tail out into a long procession as they raced for home. In the distance one could see the tide creeping over the flats, but long before it reached us there was water in the creek, so that only the sails of the boats showed moving between the banks of sand. The next fleet to look out for after the bawleys was the fleet of cockle-boats, and they would work the creek or come over the flats according to the tide. Lastly, close on high water, came the loaded barges.

From the time the young flood came up the creek to the time the tide ebbed off the flats there was always something happening. One never woke at night and peered out but one saw the unceasing life of the sea, from the mustering of the humble bawleys in the dark to go shrimping to the passing of the liner, shining from stem to stern, perhaps carrying a Viceroy to the East. Often I said to myself: 'Here I am on deck in the night, and I ought to be asleep. But it is worth it. Just think ; I might be sleepless in a house in a town, and have to look out upon a gas-lamp in a street.'

And then the entrancing variations of the tides ! What is the secret of this curiosity that compels me to come frequently on deck even in the night

A FLOATING HOME

to see whether the tide is higher or lower than it ought to be ? It is the uncertainty of what will happen, and one's partial ignorance of the causes of whatever does happen. Nautical almanacs give you their explanations of abnormalities, but they add instances of peculiar tides which are in contradiction of all their explanations. Any encyclopædia tells you that the sun and moon govern the tides ; that the moon's influence is two and a quarter times that of the sun ; that spring tides occur just after full moon and the change of the moon, and rise higher and fall lower than neap tides, which occur at the moon's quarters. But when you know that, how little you know ! The very next step takes you into one of the least accurate of sciences.

In his famous ' Wrinkle ' Captain Lecky says that we must wait for a genius to elucidate some of the mysteries. In the accounts of tides and tidal streams in nautical almanacs or the Admiralty Tide Tables one comes across phenomena about which the best authorities can say only : ' These peculiarities are probably due to . . .' Of the double low water at Weymouth Captain Lecky writes that it is not to be explained, but adds characteristically that someone has ' had a shot at it ' in the Admiralty Tide Tables. The double high water at Southampton, the twelve-foot rise to the westward of the Bristol Channel, which increases to twenty-seven feet at Lundy Island and forty feet at Bristol, and the

A FLOATING HOME

Severn bore, are easy to understand from the shape of the land. But that there should be only a six to seven foot rise on the English coast by the Isle of Wight, while there is a sixteen to seventeen foot rise on the French coast opposite, is not so simple.

Apart from peculiarities of their own in normal weather, tides are affected by strong winds and a low barometer, and then the tide tables, with their rise and fall to an inch and their time of high water to a minute, become hopelessly inaccurate. A strong north-north-west gale in the North Sea will raise the surface two or three feet and make the tides run longer on the flood ; a strong south-east or south-west wind has the opposite effect. A low glass and a strong south-west wind will make big tides at the entrance of the Channel by Plymouth. On October 14, 1881, a large mail-steamer was unable to dock at the East India Docks, London, because a severe westerly gale had kept the tide back, so that at high water it was five or six feet below its proper level, and the next flood came up three hours before its time. In January of the same year a tide was registered at London four feet ten inches above high-water mark. At Liverpool there is a record of a tide six feet above 'H.W.O.S.,' which is the abbreviation for 'high water ordinary springs.' At Milford Haven in January, 1884, during a heavy westerly gale, the tide stopped falling two hours before the proper time for low water, and at

A FLOATING HOME

low-water time had risen fifteen feet. So great is the contrariness of the tides that even strong winds cannot be relied upon for their effects.

For those whose reclaimed marshes lie behind low sea-walls in Essex the irregularities of the tides are too exciting at times. After the fierce gale in November, 1897, had veered from south-west to north-west, innumerable breaches were made in the sea-walls of the East Coast estuaries and many marshes ' went to sea.' Watchers on Latchingdon Hill, which overlooks the archipelago between the Crouch and the Thames, saw a memorable sight that day. With the shift of wind the atmosphere had cleared, and the shores of Kent were visible. At the time of high water there was a big tide, and the flood was still running strong, and continued for nearly two hours beyond its proper time. Suddenly great streaks of white appeared along the east side of Foulness Island. It was the tide pouring over the sea-walls. Havengore Island, New England Island, Rushley, and Potton Islands disappeared save for the solitary farmhouses standing in the water, and an occasional knoll crowded with frightened beasts. Then the tide flowed over the sea-walls of the Roach River and across Wallasea Island to the River Crouch. Finally, little Bridgemarsh Island and the North Fambridge marshes for two miles to the west of it disappeared, the tide rolled up to the edge of the high ground, and the sea seemed to stretch from Kent to the foot of Latchingdon Hill.

With all practical observers the turn of the tide is the critical and significant moment; it is then that the auspices are good or bad. Smacksmen tell you that if it begins to rain at high water it will continue for the whole of the ebb. They will say to one another, ' I doubt that'll rain the ebb daown,' or ' We're a goin' to have an ebb's rain.' If it begins to rain at low water they say that they will have a ' coarse flood.' Again, on a calm summer morning, if it is high water at seven or eight, and the wind then springs up easterly, there will be an easterly wind all day. But if the tide is a midday one there will be no wind till high water. Sometimes it will blow freshly at high water when there has been no wind before, and though there may be none afterwards.

Fishermen who have got ashore on a sandbank in a bit of a sea declare that they can tell at once whether the tide is ebbing or flowing by the way the vessel bumps. On the flood-tide the sand is alive, but on the ebb it is dead and as hard as flint. Ask them for an explanation, and they will retort with further facts, such as that in a calm on the flood-tide the sand can be seen boiling up in the water, but never on the ebb. Again, they believe that frost checks the tides. They say it ' nips' them—a play upon the word ' neap,' which they use as a verb, and pronounce ' nip.' Dredgermen on the River Crouch

A FLOATING HOME

will tell you that in winter, after a flood-tide with
the wind easterly, the bottom of the river is 'shet
daown hard as a road,' and the dredges slide over
the bottom and will not lift the oysters. They cannot
explain it. Undoubtedly an onshore wind and a
flood-tide bring sand into the lower reaches, for the
men find it in the dredges. On the other hand, some
declare that the bed of the river is often hardened,
where no sand is, as much as twelve miles from the
sea.

No wonder that the tides are for the fishermen the
standard of reference in all their conversation. They
will say that such-and-such a thing happened about
an hour before high water, or that the skipper of the
Ladybird went ashore just as the vessels were
swinging to the flood. If a skipper is asked when he
is going to get under way, he will say, 'As soon as
the tide serves'; or if asked why he did not arrive
before, he will answer, 'I could not save my tide.'

CHAPTER XVIII

'From Bermuda's reefs ; from edges
       Of sunken ledges,
    In some far-off, bright Azore ;
    From Bahama and the dashing,
          Silver flashing
    Surges of San Salvador.'

In August of our first summer afloat, we went for a month's cruise on the Essex coast. We had various mishaps of the kind which arrive out of the blue and remind the yachtsman that, however long his experience, he is still a learner.

One day, beating down the Colne in a fresh wind and a buffeting short sea, I made an error of judgment by sailing between two anchored barges where there was not enough room to handle the *Ark Royal*. Finding myself in difficulties, I let go the anchor, but we dragged on to one of the barges and bumped against her as gently as our best fend-offs would let us. Our anchor had fouled the other barge's cable, and it took some time to clear it, even with the help of the friendly skipper of the barge we had bumped.

164

THE RIVER ORWELL

A FLOATING HOME

' Aren't that the little ould *Will Arding*, sir ?' he said, when we were ready to drop astern and let go.

' Yes.'

' I reckoned that was she as soon as I seed 'er, and ain't she smart with her enamel and all ? But I'd a knaowed she anywhere. Scores and scores o' times she's laid alongside o' we, that she hev !'

No damage was done except to my feelings. But the barge skipper had the delicacy to say that the *Ark Royal* had meant to rub noses with an old friend, and had dragged alongside on purpose.

At Pin Mill Louisa had the panic of her life. We were all on shore except Louisa, and a shift of wind blew the stern of the anchored *Ark Royal* on to the mud. As the tide fell the barge's bows sank lower and lower until, to Louisa's horror, water began to rise over the kitchen floor. Seeing the water rise continually, she naturally thought the vessel had sprung a leak and was going to sink. Her first idea was to lift the plug to let the water out—a thing she had seen me do when the ship was high and dry. But luckily she could not get at it. With some presence of mind she then went on deck and hailed a neighbouring barge, whose skipper and mate came off and helped her to bail out her kitchen, and explained to her that as a barge is flat-bottomed the pumps can never empty her completely, and a very thin layer of water spread over such a large surface will seem considerable when it runs to one end.

A FLOATING HOME

Life moves slowly in Pin Mill. If going by steamer to Ipswich or Harwich one is expected to be seated in the ferry-boat, which goes out to meet the steamer, at least ten minutes before she starts. When we went to Ipswich one day the ferry-man, having stowed us and the other passengers in the boat, left us and returned fifty yards up the hard to resume varnishing a boat. When we did start it was certainly five minutes earlier than necessary, and we had not got more than half-way out when I saw a look of annoyance come into the ferry-man's face.

'There yaou are,' he said angrily, jerking his hand towards some figures on the shore ; 'them people tould me they wanted to go to Ipswich, and they came daown half an hour agoo, and they 'adn't got nawthen to do, only wait, and they goo off for a walk or suthen !'

Another day the children's gramophone nearly caused a fire on board to be more serious than it need have been, for it prevented us from hearing the cries for help which Louisa uttered while she struggled with an outbreak in the forecastle. We had bought a new cooking-stove with a patent automatic oil feed. We ought to have understood when buying it that it would be unsuitable because it had to be kept upright. The first time it was used while we were under way was one day in Harwich Harbour. We had been running, and had just hauled our wind to stand up the Orwell.

A FLOATING HOME

Luncheon was almost ready. The *Ark Royal* was heeling a little to a fine topsail breeze, and was spanking along to a selection from the 'Mikado,' when suddenly I saw some smoke issuing from the forehatch. I sent one of the boys forward to see what was happening, and he bellowed back that the forecastle was on fire. The Mate took the wheel, and I rushed forward in time to see Louisa, like a pantomime demon, pop up through the forehatch in a cloud of smoke. We attacked the fire from aft, and a few buckets of water and some damp sacking put it out.

In September we returned to Newcliff, went into our old berth in the creek, and once more spent Christmas on board.

Soon afterwards the Mate was taken mysteriously ill. The doctor asked for another opinion, and a specialist came from London. But for the fact of our isolation on board ship the diagnosis would instantly have been typhoid. But the next two days, we were told, would settle the question.

It was typhoid.

The ship now became a hospital, with a special bed sent down from London and two nurses. The saloon was emptied of everything save what the nurses wanted, and the long struggle began.

It was like all other serious illnesses in any other home—the children sent away, the pitiful lies that affection devises, the assumed bravery, the broken nights, the anxious talks with the nurses or doctor, and (the background of it all) the fever chart. I wonder whether any skipper of a ship ever watched his positions on a chart with such feelings as I had then.

The crisis came and passed, but ' When will she be out of danger ?' was asked secretly for many days before a confident answer came. How far these good nurses perjured themselves I do not know. Often they made me go to London, but the journey home was torture. Once, returning in the dark, I saw from the train that there was no light in the saloon. The Mate, as it turned out, was only sleeping. But afterwards a light was always placed on deck to show me that all was well.

At last the children were allowed to come and look fearfully through the windows, and later to speak a few words through them. And then step by step the Mate grew stronger until at last she walked on deck, and we dressed the ship in her honour, and she went away on a long convalescence.

When she came back well and strong I had a surprise for her. She had always been rather afraid of the great fifty-foot sprit which used to sway in a heavy threatening way over our heads when the barge rolled in a cross sea. I had therefore sold the mainsail, sprit, topsail, and mizzen, bought a large yacht's mainsail second-hand, and had it made into a new mainsail and topsail. I had also bought an eight tonner's mainsail, which I rigged as a larger mizzen. The whole transaction from first to last cost about eight pounds.

What we really needed most was a motor-launch to give the barge steerage way in calms, to help her up creeks, or for going on shore. With a slow large craft it generally happens that one has to anchor a long way off the landing-place, because the smaller craft are always near the hard ; and in bad weather this means heavy work. We bought a book on internal combustion engines, but it did not prevent us from buying an engine that did not generally achieve internal combustion.

When the next August holidays came we were delayed in starting for our usual cruise because the motor-boat had not been delivered. We stood over her till she was ready, and then went for a trial trip, during which she emitted the most distressing noises we had ever heard. However, we could wait no longer, and took her in tow behind the *Ark Royal*.

The first night of the cruise we lay off Southend. The weather, which had been bad, became worse ; the wind backed with vicious determination at low water ; and by ten o'clock it was blowing a gale. Southend is an exposed anchorage, and we foresaw that we should have some anxious hours as the tide rose. We were close to the pier, where there were five other barges, whose anchors lay round about us sticking up out of the hard sand, and promising us destruction if we should sit on one of them.

We laid out another anchor, forcing it well into the sand, and by eleven o'clock the *Ark Royal* was afloat. It was a wild night indeed; the barge wallowed, and the motor-boat jerked about on the rollers, snatched and snubbed at her painter, while the spray was cut off from the tops of the waves as though by a knife and flung into her.

I was on deck all night. The gale was blowing its worst about two o'clock in the morning at high water. I could have sworn that the other barges had driven nearer to the *Ark Royal*, so close did their flickering lights seem to us, till I checked our position by the marks I had taken and by the anchor buoys of the barges, and made sure that none of us was dragging. On board each of the barges I could discern a dim watching figure. What an incredible waste of riven water as I looked over the plunging bows of the *Ark Royal!* The sea was like a snow-drift, and across this bleak waste the wind roared unresisted and tossed the spray even on to the deck of the *Ark Royal.* I was much occupied with the thought of a humiliating wreck on a lee shore, as I had little hope of being able to claw off the land if we did begin to drive. And yet I do not think there was a moment when I would have admitted that I had chosen a wrong way of living to be here with my family instead of in a house on the land.

A FLOATING HOME

Every moment was enriched by an exhilaration that conquered other feelings, a kind of zest in defiance.

The wind is a grand enemy. He gives you his warnings fairly, and those who are not careless have generally time to cut and run if they are only coasting. In this storm, for instance, no one could have mistaken the signs. The glass had fallen rapidly, and a 'mizzle' of rain had been followed by a downpour ; and all the time the wind had been fly-ing round against the sun. The glass fell still more during the first four hours of the gale, then it suddenly leaped upwards, and the wind moderated or 'sobbed,' as the fishermen say, only to be followed by a harder blow than ever—a blow in which the squalls moved at over sixty miles an hour and followed one another in rapid succession, show-ing that the gale was still young.

There is nothing that relates the dweller at home so intimately to the business of the wider waters as to lie at the mouth of a great estuary. Here were steamers from the ends of the world slogging across the snow-drift, their masthead lights moving steadily like major planets across the sky. Some, perhaps, had passed through the very region in which this storm had been born. No yachtsman who studies the weather can think of a gale as an accident of the British Isles ; he sees in imagination a tiny cyclone created as a whirlwind somewhere, it may be, in six to eight degrees north latitude. In the desert of the Atlantic,

A FLOATING HOME

in calm and heat, with the sun nearly overhead, a tiny column of air ascends and cooler air rushes in to replace it. The cyclone is born. Perhaps it is not a hundred yards across, but as it goes revolving on its journey of thousands of miles it draws in the air all round it as a snowball gathers snow. Westward and north-westward it travels to the West Indies, turning on its axis against the hands of a watch, unlike the cyclone born south of the equator, which revolves the other way. The wind does not blow accurately around the centre, but curves inwards spirally, so that in the northern hemisphere, when you stand face to wind, the centre of the storm is always from eight to twelve points to the right.

When once you understand this rotatory and spiral movement of the wind you cannot listen to the roar of a gale without thinking of ocean-going sailing ships fleeing from the deadly centre. You think of the cyclone touching the West Indies : one rim on the islands, the palm-trees staggering at the assault ; the other rim on the open ocean, a ship laid over by the blast, the crew, clinging to the yards, fighting to get the maddened canvas under control before it is too late. The master of that ship had had the warning of the swell which is the gentle forerunner of the storm, but perhaps he carried on too long. Now, under heavily reefed canvas, or perhaps under bare poles, he races from the deadly centre of the storm.

A FLOATING HOME

From the West Indies the storm curves to the northward and north-eastward, still growing in size, till it may have a diameter of even a thousand miles. Along the Gulf Stream it comes, conveying within its frame that mysterious core which no one in a sailing ship ever wishes to see—a central patch, it is said, of unnatural calm surrounded by squalls from every point of the compass, a patch where the sea is piled up into a pyramid, untrue, treacherous, and overwhelming. The cyclone bursts later into that tract of dripping fog where the Gulf Stream meets her frigid sister from the north ; and when it reaches us in England it is sometimes huge and harmless, but sometimes it has stored its strength and blares across a comparatively narrow belt with the power of a hurricane. And it comes in various guises, in pale bright skies, or wreathed in films of scud, or in rolling hard-edged clouds of inky darkness, or behind a tormented veil of rain.

About three o'clock in the morning I went below to drink some tea and to smoke. When I returned the motor-boat was gone. The frayed painter, hanging from the stern of the *Ark Royal*, told me what had happened. Our brand-new uninsured motor-boat, which we never ought to have bought ! I knew that if she had reached the stone-faced sea-wall or one of the breakwaters there was little hope for her.

As the tide fell I went off in the dinghy in search

A FLOATING HOME

of her. Fortunately, I found her in the hands of two men from the gasworks, who had seen her coming ashore and had waded out to meet her. They had pushed her clear of a breakwater, and were standing in the rollers holding her head to sea at the foot of the sea-wall.

As the tide fell farther we walked her out gradually to the *Ark Royal*, and I settled the question of salvage by paying a couple of pounds. Even Cockney Smith could not have accused the gas-workers of a 'salvage job' in the circumstances, though no doubt he would have pointed out that they were gas-workers and not sailormen.

Our cruise of that summer was ordered by the necessity of sailing continually from one port where there was a motor engineer to another port where there was another engineer. The children used to take the metal seals off the petrol cans and hang them on the engine as medals, in numbers according to the merit of its performance. If the engine began to knock, for instance, a medal would be forfeited —to be restored if the knocking stopped. They enjoyed the vagaries of the engine; and loved it in secret even when it stopped work altogether and had lost all its decorations. They christened the motor-boat *Perhaps*.

CHAPTER XIX

'The stormy evening closes now in vain,
Loud wails the wind and beats the driving rain,
While here in sheltered house,
With fire-ypainted walls,
I hear the wind abroad,
I hear the calling squalls—
"Blow, blow !" I cry; "you burst your cheeks in vain !
Blow, blow !" I cry; "my love is home again !"'

AFTER the Mate's illness an unreasoning dread of the place where she had lain ill conquered me, and I put away all idea of returning there for the winter. Fortunately, a move was easy enough. If we had been living in a house it would have been otherwise, but a 'house removal' for us meant no more than weighing anchor and going to a new spot of our choice. Our choice was conditioned, first, by the necessity of my going to London daily ; and, secondly, by the need of providing for our girl's education, who was now of school-going age.

One anchorage—now known to us as the Happy Haven—attracted us beyond all others. We had found it under stress of weather during one of our Essex cruises, and had ever since thought of it with affection for the quiet peace of the tidal creek between its grassy banks and for the welcome we had received from the family which lives at the head of that creek and presides over its amenities.

As the autumn deepened it became urgently necessary to decide upon our winter quarters, but the Mate had received no answer to a letter in which she had asked the Lady at the Happy Haven whether means of education for Margaret could be found thereabouts. One day, when we had almost despaired of an answer, I met the father of the family at the Happy Haven unexpectedly in London. His wife, he said, had been travelling; we must write again. And soon an answer came that solved our difficulties. There was no school to give such an education as we wanted, but Margaret could be taught with the family in the house at the head of the Happy Haven. Within a few days we sailed to the Happy Haven, and there we have since lived and hope long to live.

To reach our port there are but two ways, one by water and one by land. Are you coming by water? Then you must come in from the sea and take the young flood up the river past the low-lying islands ; if the wind be foul you will have to wait for water according to your draught. With a fair wind come straight on past the village and the wood off which the smacks lie, and past the church tower to the south. When abreast the creek leading to the red-

A FLOATING HOME

tiled farmhouse on the starboard hand you will find the best water in the middle.

Keep close to the point on the north side, and from there steer straight for the three great poplars you will see ahead until you reach another church among the trees on the north side. Then keep the hut on the point just open of the old water-mill.

It is quite easy. But long before you come to the Happy Haven our mahogany-faced old pilot, with a walk like a penguin, a parson's hat tied under his chin with a piece of tarred string, a red jumper, and yellow fearnought trousers, will 'board you,' if you want him, and berth you. Two shillings is his charge.

But suppose you come by land. For two shillings you can be driven from the railway station out through the old market town until you come to an avenue of trees and a rookery. There you must turn off the public road into a private road, and drive under the great trees which meet above, and down a lane of thorns until, suddenly turning a corner, you will drive alongside the river to the grassy quay where the *Ark Royal* is lying.

You can go no farther, for the road ends there.

After all, you may say, there is not much to see. Only an old water-mill and three barges alongside it ; the mill-house, and above it the mill-head spreading wide ; our friend's house among the poplars ; on the opposite shore a farmhouse where

A FLOATING HOME

a barge is loading hay ; under the sea-walls on both sides fields dotted with cattle and white gulls ; an unbroken vault of sky; and the shining creek stretching away into the ultimate green of flat pasture lands. Perhaps a red-sailed barge is coming up the river; the 'tuke,' or redshanks, are giving warning of her approach ; and a thousand dunlin keep settling on the brown mud, rising to show off all together in a flash that they are snow white underneath.

A cable's length from the *Ark Royal* is a small head of water held up by a sea-wall and a sluice-gate, and from it, meandering down past the ship into the gut, is a narrow course worn by the water. If you happen to come at the right moment, two families of children in bathing costumes—ours and the children from the house among the poplars—will be taking turns at packing themselves into a large bath. Someone lifts the gate, and the bath in a torrent of foamy water 'chutes' down the channel into the gut or is capsized on the way.

Such is a brief description of how to arrive at the Happy Haven, and what there is to see there. But wild tugs with steel hawsers will not drag the name from me. Those who want to live in floating homes will search far to find a better berth.

We have only one very near neighbour, an ex-barge skipper. Like the bargee of whom Stevenson wrote, there seems to be no reason why he should not live

A FLOATING HOME

for ever. He has seen the best part of eighty years,
and is still hearty and quite as active as he need be.
He has achieved an appearance barely suitable to old
age, and has stopped there. He spends many hours
each day in thought. Like us, he pays no rent, rates,
or taxes, for he lives in a small and old yacht. And
though his means of living are a mystery he lives
well.

Twice to our knowledge he has taken a party for
a short cruise in the yacht, but beyond this we
have never known him earn a penny. And yet if a
new mast be wanted, or new iron work, or paint,
or varnish, or a rope for fitting out, or a new sail,
he buys it. Rumour says he has been a notable
smuggler, and there are some that say he has friends
who are still free traders. Others believe that he has
a share in a barge. But no one knows.

Always healthy, he observes none of the laws of
health. It is true he sleeps nine hours every night,
but that is in a cabin without ventilation. On a fine
summer's morning most people, when they get up,
begin to do something, even though it be unimportant. Not so our friend. He starts the day—breaking, as usual, some rule of health—by lighting his
pipe. Then, seating himself comfortably in the open,
he airs himself for a long time. While the airing is
going on he surveys the sky many times, rotating
slowly till he has examined all points of the compass. If anyone be present, he will give his con-

sidered verdict on the prospects of the weather for the day.

When that problem has been solved he will chop a few sticks and remark that he must ' see about his kittle.' Soon afterwards smoke will issue from the chimney of his boat, and for the next hour he will not be visible. After that some cleaning operations— not personal—will go on in the cockpit for possibly another hour. Then he may scrape a spar or varnish one, or do a bit of painting. If it be hot he will probably rig an awning, and sit beneath it stitching at an old sail; if it be cold he will rig up a windscreen, and sit behind that.

A couple of hours before high water the pilot, also an ex-barge skipper, arrives to see what barges are coming up, and then he and our friend will be seen side by side discussing things connected with the sea. The approaching barges have to be watched until recognized, and again watched until they are safely berthed. From this important but unpaid labour they know no remission during the proper hours.

Thus, with intervals for meals, our curious neighbour passes his days from one end of the year to the other.

Sometimes I have had the privilege of being present at the sessions of our neighbour and the pilot. One day the pilot described the sorrows of fishermen when the stinging jelly-fish are about, for he spends an odd day at sea in a smack.

A FLOATING HOME

'The water's full o' they blessed ould stingin' squalders, and every time us hauls aour net that's full on 'em, and they do make me swear suthen. That ain't a mite o' use tryin' to be religious, same as if you wants to be, with them stingin' squalders abaout. They're puffect devils.'

I remember the pilot's comment on our neighbour's account of a hailstorm. 'That was a wonnerful heavy hailstorm, that was,' said our neighbour, 'and the stones was most as big as acorns. And one come and hit me on the laower part of the thumb. Lor', that did hurt suthen !'

'Well, that come a long way, yer see,' said the pilot.

Another day the pilot, who is appreciably more mobile than our neighbour, described to me an errand of mercy he had undertaken.

'I've just been daown to see pore ould George what bruk his arm last week. Yaou know him, sir, don't ye ? Him what's skipper of the *Nancy*. I wonder who'll sail she while 'is arm's a mendin'. Wonnerful venturesome fellow is George, and that's haow 'e come to do ut. He took and bought one o' they bicycles. From what I can hear of it, 'e larnt to ride that well enough same as on the flat. They what taught he to ride tould he to shorten sail same as goin' daown hills and that, and maybe 'e did. But accordin' to what I can hear of it, that bicycle took charge daown the hill just past the railway, and

A FLOATING HOME

George den't fare to knaow what to do, so 'e reckoned that were best to thraow she up in the wind. And they picked the ould fellow out o' the ditch with his arm bruk. 'E's gettin' on well, and is all right in 'is 'ealth. The doctor's a givin' of him some of that medicine aout o' one o' they raound bottles.'

Besides his boat our neighbour owns a shed. When he applied originally to the landowner for leave to put up the shed he was refused, because the landowner feared that it would be unsightly. The negotiations that followed are a model for diplomacy.

The old man next asked that he might be allowed to haul up an ancient sieve-like boat on to the bank. To this the landowner assented—if it could be done, which he doubted.

It was done.

But at very high tides the ground underneath the overturned boat was flooded, so that gear stored there could not be kept dry. The boat was then raised bodily a foot or so from the ground by planking. After a few weeks, to make more storage room still, the old man raised the sides of his boat some three feet more and put a roof over her.

This structure escaped objection from the landowner for a year, and so the following summer the roof was removed, the sides were raised another two feet, and the roof was put on again.

This also escaped criticism. Accordingly, the

A FLOATING HOME

following year an annexe was built on at the bows, and eventually a cement floor was laid. Now there is a water-butt at the junction of the annexe and the main building.

We await further developments.

We made the mistake once—if, indeed, it was not an offence—of offering our neighbour some work. He explained that he had too much to do already, and referred to a particular job which he did not begin till six months later. 'No sooner do I git one job done than I sees another starin' me in the face,' he often says.

Last summer he painted the inside of his yacht, and for ten days he slept in his boat-hut on shore. Sundown every evening was his time for 'bunkin' up,' as he called it, and we used to make a point of asking him what time he would be up in the morning. To this he would answer: 'Abaout five or six, I reckon. Last summer I used to get up at faour sometimes. Goo to bed with the ould hens and git up along of 'em—that's the way.'

Then we would watch him retire. There is no door on hinges to his hut, but a flap which fits in the opening. He had to disappear stern first, fit the flap in the bottom of the opening, and pull the top into position with a string. He withdrew from our gaze each evening in the following order : legs, body clad in a blue jersey, white beard, red face, and straw hat.

A FLOATING HOME

The next morning we would always be up first, and while we were busy on deck we kept an eye open for the first trembling of the flap. Then out would come the hat, the red face, the white beard, blue body, and legs, and another day had begun for our neighbour. We thought he would have made excuses for not getting up earlier, but we soon discovered that on most days he had no idea what the time was.

At the Happy Haven our water is brought to us by cart in a canvas water-carrier, which holds two hundred gallons. One day we had a panic about one of the tanks. The water-cart had brought four loads, and still the tanks were not full. We heard a sound of running water, which we took to be the water siphoning from one tank to the other. When I returned from London the next evening, the sound of running water continued, but there was something worse—an audible splashing. And the water in the port tank had fallen. Friends were dining with us that night, but luckily they did not expect conventional amusements; they preferred tackling leaking water-tanks to bridge.

The first thing to be done was to break the siphon between the two tanks by letting air into the pipe. After trying in vain to unscrew a joint I decided to drill a small hole in the pipe; but, using more force than skill, I broke my only drill. This meant that all the water still in the tanks—six hundred gallons—

A FLOATING HOME

might find its way into the bilge. We pulled up a floor-board aft, and discovered that the missing water was even then nearly level with the floor. I lifted the plug aft, but the water would not run out, as the barge was sitting on soft mud, which choked the hole. Pumping is back-breaking work, and I did not intend to do that if it could be avoided. I put on sea-boots and went over the side with a boat-hook and a kind of hoe to puggle about until there was a clear way for the water to run. The difficulty was to find the hole, but the ladies held lights and called out directions while the men shoved a stick through the plug-hole. The water began to run at last, and the *Ark Royal* was soon dry.

The next day we emptied the port tank into the bilge, and the plumber got inside through the man-hole and found the hole, which by a great piece of luck was in such a position that he could mend it by removing enough of the bathroom bulkhead to allow his hand to get through. What we should have done if the hole had been out of reach we hardly dared to think.

Many of our friends have said that they would like to live in the *Ark Royal* in the summer, but most of them boggle at the thought of the winter. To me, somehow, the contrast between the comfortable interior of our home and the rigours of the winter scene pressing close in upon us is particularly satisfying. It is very agreeable at the end of

A FLOATING HOME

a winter's day in London to come back to the barge ;
to leave an office with its telephone bells, and
the hubbub of the streets ; to come in little more
than an hour to where the lane of thorns ends at the
sea-wall. The faint glow ahead comes from the *Ark
Royal.* Those piping cries are the redshanks calling
in the dark. As I come nearer the separate columns
of light from the windows and skylights beam like
searchlights. And above the blaze stands up the
mast and rigging, free from all burden and strain,
resting the winter through. The cheerful chimneys
pour out their smoke, which, blowing darkly to leeward, turns into clouds of misty gold as it crosses the
belt of yellow light.

Even in our retired creek it is a joy to know that
we are on the magic road, which is all roads in the
world because it leads everywhere. Of course, we
shall never sail out to the back of beyond ; but
when on summer nights we sit on deck under the
pole star, and the phosphorescent water streams past
our side like molten metal, we feel that the same sea
that bears us laps equatorial islands and continents.

When the *Ark Royal* lifts to the rising tide
her timbers creak as though she were asking to be
free ; and her voice is high or low according to the
wind. At night she speaks most clearly. In measure
to the wind she reminds us of peaceful driftings
under still skies, or of torn sails and dragging anchors.
When a gale with all the weight of winter behind

A FLOATING HOME

it bursts in squalls through the rigging, the tiny waves of our haven rip along our sides and the lamp in the saloon swings gently. Then we know, at a safe remove, what weather there must be 'outside' if we have such tumult in here. Heaven help us if we were out in the Swin with those clean-bowed fish-carriers that are racing in from the North Sea! Let us hope that the barges that have been 'caught' have reached such anchorages as Abraham's Bosom, or the Blacktail Swatch, sheltered from clumsy steamers by the lighthouse and from the weather by the sand.

Even my insurance policy recognizes that our life is not as life on shore. I am 'Master under God of and in the good ship or vessel called the *Ark Royal.*' And the policy deals with life in a large way. For example : ' Touching the perils whereof they, the assurers, are content to bear, they are of the Seas, Men of War, Fire, Pirates, Rovers, Thieves, Jettisons, Letters of Mart and Countermart, Surprisals, Takings at Sea, Arrests, Restraints and Detainments of all Kings, Princes and People of what Nation, Condition, or Quality soever, Barratry of the Master and Mariners and of all other Perils and Losses.'

*　　*　　*　　*　　*

Several years have we spent in the *Ark Royal*, and let it be admitted that we feel the need for more room. Once more perceive the advantage of living afloat. We can add to our establishment in units.

A FLOATING HOME

No builders will tear down our creepers, or excavate our garden, or mix mortar on the lawn. Nor shall we suffer the horrid noise of carpenters. When our additional rooms are ready they will be floated alongside. No District Council will have a word to say about the material of the new building or the nature of the roof.

The *Overdraft*, as our first addition under the unitary system is called—a name which is nautical in sound, and suggests both the overflowing of the ship's company and a certain financial operation at the bank—is an old lighter thirty-five feet long with a beam of twelve feet. We are raising her sides to a height of seven feet six inches and dividing her into three compartments. There will be a sleeping-cabin at each end, and the middle room will be a workshop and playroom, fitted with a carpenter's bench and a range for both cooking and heating. If our friends in the house among the poplars give a dance we shall be able to float the *Overdraft* along to the foot of their garden to provide extra rooms for their guests. When she lies alongside the *Ark Royal* there will be a covered-in gangway to her entrance-door.

Some day, by the unitary system, we may add other rooms, but the only plan in the offing which seems reasonably likely to reach port soon is a scheme for electric lighting by using our head of water to drive the dynamo.

A FLOATING HOME

The reader may permit, however, a vision of our ultimate development. We have often desired to own a tug—having long been strong admirers of the indescribable fussiness and importance of tugs. We should keep steam up in our tug, and use her at moorings as a central heating plant. We should offer to tow the trading barges in and out of the creek, which would be one of the best pastimes imaginable, besides bringing us many devoted friends. And then when we wanted to shift our anchorage! You should just be there to see us start: first the tug, then the *Ark Royal*, then the *Overdraft*, then the other extra rooms, then the *Perhaps*, then the sailing dinghy, and lastly the duck punt. When the moment came to anchor again there would be no orders in the manner of 'Let go the 'ook, Bill,' but a dignified signal from the tug in the way described by the best of English sea songs:

'Then the signal was made for the grand fleet to anchor.'

APPENDIX

DETAILS OF THE COST OF BUYING, ALTERING, AND FITTING OUT THE *ARK ROYAL*

	£	s.	d.
Purchase	140	0	0
Wood, match-lining, and flooring	37	17	7
Three-ply veneers	15	3	11
Insurance during alterations, £2 ; Registration, £1 1s. ; Changing name, £3 18s.	6	19	0
Galvanizing chain, stanchions, blacksmith's work ...	8	15	9
Two tanks of 400 gallons each...	8	0	0
Six mahogany doors and other fittings from ship-breaker's yard	5	4	6
Pumps, bath, w.c., heating stove for bath... ...	13	16	7
Brass fittings, tools, and sundries	4	15	11
Paint and varnish	6	5	8
Rope	5	8	8
Disinfecting at gasworks : formaldehyde, etc. ...	4	2	6
Kitchen range, copper, etc.	6	0	0
Linoleum, wash-hand-stand, brass fittings ...	6	5	0
Plumbing	7	16	0
Raising main cabin-top	38	10	0
Wages : two men for four months	39	15	0
Lamps, £2 10s. ; Nails, £2 3s. ; Saloon stove, £2 10s.	7	3	0
Caulking deck and buying and fixing second-hand skylight for boys' cabin	5	12	0
Brass screws, hinges, and wire rope	3	19	0
Petty cash	4	8	11
	£375	19	0

A FLOATING HOME

A few words must be added in explanation of these bare figures.

As the cost of labour after the *Ark Royal* reached Fleetwick, with the cabin-top raised, was only £39 15s., the reader can understand how much was done by the owner's hands. Help, however, was given by friends— in particular by a retired Civil Servant who displayed extraordinary skill as a carpenter. It was a mistake not to raise the main cabin-top ourselves. We probably could have done the job better, and certainly we could have done it cheaper.

Now as regards the annual expenses of upkeep, apart from the interest on the capital sunk. These expenses, of course, do not appear in the table of initial cost. The largest item is insurance. Our policy allows us to cruise sixty-two days in the year, with a rebate for the number of days' cruising short of the allowance. The policy works out at about £10 a year. So far we have done all the annual fitting-out ourselves, the cost of which, with varnish, paint, and renewals, has averaged about £5.

Our running gear lasts a long time, as our cruises are short. We have not renewed our sails since the barge was rerigged. The sails of a trading barge, if carefully tended, last ten or twelve years. Ours, therefore, should last at least twenty. The upkeep of barges has been reduced to a science. All gear and fittings are standardized, and there is, besides, a free market in second-hand things taken out of condemned barges.

A barge's sides are tarred and blackleaded. This costs shillings where paint and anti-fouling composition would cost pounds. Although we tar and blacklead the *Ark Royal's* sides, we have a false whale which we enamel

A FLOATING HOME

white. Another economy we practise is to paint the
cabin-tops with Stockholm tar, thinned out with paraffin
and with a little teak paint to colour it. As the superficial
area of the two cabin-tops is four hundred square feet, much
paint would be required. The stanchions, the wheel, iron
uprights which hold the sidelight screens, metal blocks,
and most ironwork, we cover with galvanizing paint,
which costs little, is easily renewed, and looks smart.

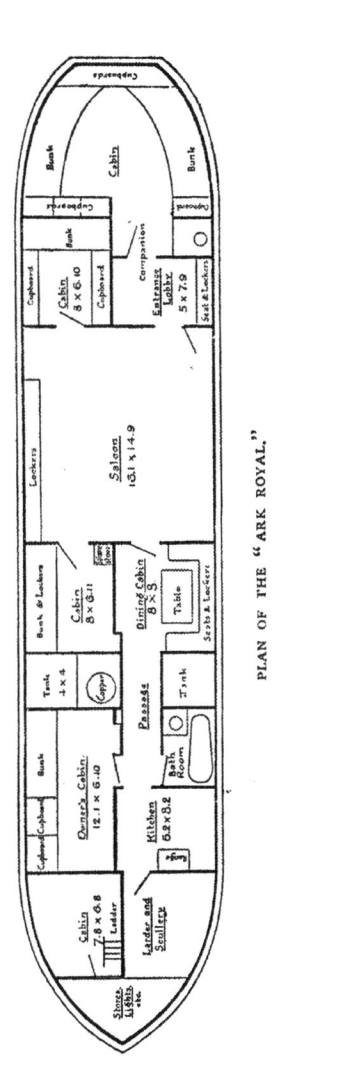

PLAN OF THE "ARK ROYAL."

A GLOSSARY OF ESSEX WORDS
AND PHRASES

In this Glossary obvious mispronunciations and corruptions are not included. By including them a glossary might be extended indefinitely, and to no profit. Numerous Essex dialect words are, of course, current in other counties ; Essex shares a particularly large number with the rest of East Anglia. The aim here is simply to give the dialect words which the authors of this book have themselves heard in Essex, and which they believe to be most characteristic. No one interested in dialect is ignorant where to turn for the greatest store of information on the subject yet collected—Dr. Joseph Wright's masterly work, *The English Dialect Dictionary*. The following list, however, contains several words which do not appear in that Dictionary. The dictionary is referred to as *E. D. D.* :

Bangy (pronounced 'banjy'), drizzling, misty. 'Bange' is a very light rain.

Between lights, twilight.

Bever, light refreshments between the larger meals, eaten either at 11 a.m. or 4 p.m. (*Cf.* 'levenses' and 'levener,' which are the same words as 'elevens' and 'elevener,' meaning a slight meal eaten at eleven in the morning. *Cf.* also 'fours' or 'fourses,' which is a similar meal eaten about four o'clock in the afternoon.)

Bibble, to tipple ; to drink noisily like a duck.

Bird, pupil of the eye.

Blare, to cry, blubber.

Botty, conceited.

Breeder, abscess, boil.

A FLOATING HOME

Bulk, to throb (the ' u ' pronounced as in ' bull '). Also **Bullock.**

Buller, *vide* **Duller** (the ' u ' pronounced as in ' dull ').

Bullock, another form of ' bulk.'

Buskins, gaiters.

Buzz, blow on the head. (Not in *E. D. D.*)

Cankerhooks, tenterhooks. (Not in *E. D. D.*)

Chance time, sometimes.

Chissick, pinch (of salt, pepper, sugar, or suchlike). (Not in *E. D. D.*)

Choice, pinch (of salt, pepper, sugar, or suchlike). (Not in *E. D. D.*)

Coarse, rough. Used of the weather. A fisherman will say, in a curious phrase, ' Coarse weather, don't it ?'

Coase, to pet, stroke—*e.g.*, ' he was coasing his dog.' The ' s ' is pronounced as in ' roast.' (Not in *E. D. D.*) The word no doubt comes from the same root as the well-known word *cosset.*

Cob, long basket, manure-hod.

Cotchel. A barge is said to go cotchelling when she discharges or takes up her cargo piecemeal at various ports, instead of taking a single cargo from one port to another. *E. D. D.* gives the substantive ' cotchel,' meaning an odd measure or a partially filled sack, but does not mention the verb which has been formed from this word.

Court, stye—*e.g.*, ' hogs' court,' ' pigs' court.'

Crock, smudge of soot, smut.

Cuff, tall story. (*E. D. D.* gives *cuffer.*)

Cuff, to tell tall stories—*e.g.*, ' He's cuffin' a rare yarn.'

Culch, rubbish. Particularly, in fishermen's language, the broken shells of an oyster-bed.

Curren, cunning, sly. (Not in *E. D. D.*)

Dag (frequently pronounced ' daig '), dew, mist.

Deleet, cross-roads—*e.g.*, a ' three deleet ' or a ' four deleet,' according as three or four roads meet **Releet** is another form. (*E. D. D.* gives **Releet** and **Eleet.**)

Ding, to work at—*e.g.*, ' I'm dinging all the coal out o' that ould locker.' When fishermen throw their catch down into the hold, they are said to ding it. The word of command for all

A FLOATING HOME

hands to begin their work is 'Ding!' In the Essex use of the word the sense of furious effort mentioned in *E. D. D.* seems to be absent.

Discern, to see. Constantly used when there is no suggestion whatever of seeing something with an appreciable effort.

Do, used elliptically for 'if it does,' 'if he does'—*e.g.*, 'That'll rain, *do*, that'll rain hard.'

Doddy, little. Often used intensively with 'little'—*e.g.*, 'Doddy little boat.'

Doke, dent, impression.

Dooberous, doubtful, dubious, suspicious. The nearest word to this in *E. D. D.* is the Norfolk 'dooblus,' which would perhaps be better spelt 'dooblous.' An Essex fisherman will say, 'I doubt that's dooberous to go to leeward of that buoy.'

Doubt, to think, consider—*e.g.*, 'I doubt that's goin' to rain'; 'I doubt he won't catch the train.'

Draining, *vide* **Dreening.**

Dreening, wringing wet. Also **Draining.**

Dringle, to dawdle along. When the tide is barely moving it is said to be 'just dringling.'

Drizzle, to cry a little—*e.g.*, 'She kep' all on a drizzlin'.'

Duller, to moan or blubber noisily (the 'u' pronounced as in 'dull'). Also **Buller.**

Dunted, melancholy, depressed.

Dunty, stupid. Used of sheep that are difficult to drive.

Duzzy, stupid, dazed.

Fall, to drift—*e.g.*, a smack falls through a reach with her trawl down.

Fare, to do, seem. This word is the Essex maid-of-all-work. It serves as many purposes as the French *faire*, with which, however, it probably has no etymological connection.

Fleet, tidal dyke in a marsh. Any shallow dyke or ditch.

Fleet, to float. Past participle is 'flet.'

Fleet, shallow—*e.g.*, a man will 'plough fleet.' Again, a waterway is said to be fleet enough when it has fall enough for the water to flow.

Frickle, to fidget. Used of the tide swerving about in eddies.

196

A FLOATING HOME

Gag, to retch.

Good tightly, properly, well.

Grizzle, to whine, cry, complain.

Gull, scour out, especially by means of running water.

Gushy, gusty.

Haggy daggy, mist.

Happen, perhaps.

Head. This word is used to express the superlative—*e.g.*, 'a head masterpiece.'

Hoggle, to sail with easy canvas before a fair wind, or to roll in a calm with the boom swinging. The word is no doubt related to such a phrase as 'hoggling boggling,' meaning unsteady.

Hoo roo, row, fight.

Housen, houses.

Hull, to hurl, to throw.

In, often used for ' of '—*e.g.*, 'What do I think in it ?'

Jack at a pinch, man employed in an emergency—*e.g.*, man brought into a crew at the last moment.

Jown, joined, spliced.

Juble, jolly, merry. (Not in *E. D. D.*)

Kelter, condition, order. 'Out of kelter' means 'out of order.'

Kilter, *vide* **Kelter.**

Largess, extra pay, especially at harvest.

Lessest, least.

Levener, light meal between breakfast and dinner. *Vide* **Bever.**

Low, to allow, estimate, reckon.

Masterous, wonderful, astonishing. A superlative of this word is sometimes used. A man will say, ' That was the masterousest thing I ever did see.' (Not in *E. D. D.*)

Masterpiece, wonderful or astonishing thing.

Mawther, a girl.

Mizzle, light rain.

Nit, nor yet.

Nuzzle. A fisherman will say that he 'nuzzled the mud' (*i.e.*, ran the bows of his smack on the mud on the flood tide) while having his dinner.

197

A FLOATING HOME

Offer to, try to—*e.g.*, ' I was that bad winter-time I lay abed six weeks and never offered to move.'

Old. It is impossible to ascribe any particular meaning to this word. In Essex dialect it is the universal adjective.

Paffle, breaking water caused by wind and tide—*e.g.*, ' The reach was all of a paffle.' (This meaning is not mentioned in *E. D. D.*)

Paltry, poor in health.

Peak, to peep or pry—*e.g.*, ' A rabbit peaked out of its hole.'

Pingle, to be fanciful about one's food.

Pingly, off colour, having a bad appetite.

Pucker, to worry.

Pucker, agitated state of mind—*e.g.*, ' She was in a regular pucker.'

Puggle, to mess about, particularly with a stick in opening a hole stopped with rubbish. Thus, figuratively, to muddle about.

Push, boil, abscess.

Releet, *vide* **Deleet.**

Riddy, rid.

Rowels, thick stockings worn inside sea-boots. (Not in *E. D. D.*)

Same. It is impossible to give precise meanings for this word in its frequent and various uses. They may be deduced from the dialogue of this book. It may be said that in Essex dialect the word ' same ' commonly introduces a hypothetical statement which might equally well be expressed by ' supposing.' If you ask an Essex man to explain something, he will begin: ' Same as if you was doing so-and-so—'. If he imagines something happening in the winter, he will say, ' Same as winter-time.'

Scrouge, to crowd.

Scud. When fish, lying in the net alongside a smack, are shaken along to the most convenient point for lifting them on board, they are said to be scudded. Fish are also scudded into the hold.

Seizen, to bind, or seize, things together.

Shiftening, change of clothes.

Shiver, slice.

Similar-same, like.

A FLOATING HOME

Snarled, tangled, knotted.

Sneer, to twitch, wince.

Sob. When the wind dies away temporarily, it is said to 'sob' or 'sob down.'

Soo, to settle down, like a vessel on the mud that is gradually being left by the tide. (Not in *E. D. D.*)

Spuffle, to fume.

Squalder, jelly-fish. In Norfolk 'squadling' and 'swalder' mean a small jelly-fish, but among Essex fishermen 'squalder,' which seems to be a form of 'squadling,' is used of the large stinging jelly-fish. (Not in *E. D. D.*)

Stam, to astonish.

Stench, to stanch. Used of soaking a boat or barrel to make the wood swell or 'take up.'

Stetchy, *vide* **Tetchy.**

Suthen, something. Widely used as an adverb of emphasis—*e.g.*, 'That blowed suthen hard last night.'

Tempest, thunderstorm. (Not used of wind.)

Ter, it. Used in such phrases as 'as ter was' for 'as it was.' A fisherman examining a dead bird on the shore was heard to say, 'That's a watery bird be ter whether ter may'—*i.e.*, 'That's a sea-bird whatever it may be.'

Tetchy, treacherous. Used of the wind when it flies about from one point of the compass to another. Also **Stetchy.**

That. Universally used throughout Essex, as in all East Anglia, for 'it.' People say, 'That's a goin' to rain,' 'I doubt that'll turn to wind,' 'That'll be a rum 'un [*i.e.*, a strange thing] if he comes,' and so on. This is probably a relic of the old Anglo-Saxon neuter.

Thrashel, *vide* **Threscal.**

Threddle, *vide* **Thriddle.**

Threscal, threshold, door-sill. Also **Thrashel.**

Thriddle, to thread one's way as through a crowded harbour. (Not in *E. D. D.*) Also **Threddle.**

Tissick, a tickling cough.

Tore out, worn out.

To-she-from-she gate, kissing gate. (Not in *E. D. D.*)

199

A FLOATING HOME

Wanten, wanted.

Went, gone—*e.g.*, ' He ought never to have went.'

Wonderful, very—*e.g.*, ' He's a wonderful long time a comin'.'
Some Essex people use the word (like ' old,' *q.v.*) in almost
every sentence.

Wring, to strain. A barge is said to wring when she changes her
shape slightly through lying on uneven ground. When a
vessel begins to move perceptibly, without actually floating,
on the in-coming tide the fisherman says, ' She's wringing.'
This is only a special sense, of course, of the old intransitive
verb ' to wring,' meaning to writhe or twist.

BILLING AND SONS, LTD., PRINTERS, GUILDFORD, ENGLAND

Lightning Source UK Ltd.
Milton Keynes UK
UKHW050213141218
333977UK00028B/439/P